Praise for *Secrets of*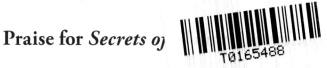

T0165488

"*Secrets of Shiksa Appeal* is not only helpful, but hysterical! Taking her cue from *The Rules*, Ms. Avi teaches women to dress for men, play hard to get, and keep men hooked. Every Jewish woman should read this book."
- Ellen Fein and Sherrie Schneider, #1 New York Times Best-Selling authors, *The Rules*

"*Secrets of Shiksa Appeal* will make you laugh, cry, or both!"
- *The Baltimore Jewish Times*

"If you ever heard the words, 'You remind me too much of my mother' from a man, you should immediately read *Secrets of Shiksa Appeal*. It will teach you how to bring out your sexy hidden shiksa while stifling your inner Jewish mother until some poor, unsuspecting mensch has actually turned you into a Jewish mother yourself!"
- Jodi Lipper, co-author of *How to Eat Like a Hot Chick, How to Love Like a Hot Chick & Live Like a Hot Chick*

"*Secrets of Shiksa Appeal* is wise, irreverent, and hilarious. Any nice Jewish girl who follows Ms. Avi's advice can catch the Jewish stallion (or near-sighted miniature horse) of her dreams and have a (matzo) ball doing it. This is a must read for Jewish single gals."
- Lori Uscher-Pines, PhD, author of the *Get Your Man to Marry You Plan*

"Ms. Avi attacks head-on the controversial Jewish dating topics most are afraid to discuss in a fun and easy-to-read format."
- Michael Karlan, author, *DC for Singles* and President of Professionals in the City

Secrets of Shiksa Appeal

Eight Steps to
Attract Your Shul-Mate

Avi Roseman

iUniverse, Inc.
Bloomington

Secrets of Shiksa Appeal
Eight Steps to Attract Your Shul-Mate

iUniverse books may be ordered through booksellers or by contacting:

iUniverse
1663 Liberty Drive
Bloomington, IN 47403
www.iuniverse.com
1-800-Authors (1-800-288-4677)

Because of the dynamic nature of the Internet, any web addresses or links contained in this book may have changed since publication and may no longer be valid. The views expressed in this work are solely those of the author and do not necessarily reflect the views of the publisher, and the publisher hereby disclaims any responsibility for them.

Any people depicted in stock imagery provided by Thinkstock are models, and such images are being used for illustrative purposes only.

Certain stock imagery © Thinkstock.

ISBN: 978-1-4502-8999-3 (sc)
ISBN: 978-1-4502-9001-2 (hc)
ISBN: 978-1-4502-9000-5 (e)

Library of Congress Control Number: 2011909315

Printed in the United States of America

iUniverse rev. date: 08/08/2011

Table of Contents

Acknowledgements: ix

Introduction: 1
Why Write About *Them*? 2
Some Basic Truths: 5
What You Will Learn: The 8-Step Method: 10
Have Faith in Our Kind: 11
Dear Ms. Avi - Dating Goyim. 14

Chapter 1—Shiksify Your Look: Be Yourself, Just Better. 15
You *Are Sexy!* 16
That's Nice, Ms. Avi, But... 17
A Grand List of What Men Find Attractive About Women: . . .17
Shiksas Don't Wear Schmatas! 19
Look Cute in Unsuspecting Places: 21
What to Wear on a Date: 22
Dear Ms. Avi - Heels 25

Chapter 2—Playing Hard to Get, Shiksa Style. 26
You're Jewish Too? Great, I'm Gonna Throw Myself at You: . . 27
Study Her: 28
Don't Chase—Let Them Come After You: 29
Learn to Receive—Ask Not What You Can Do for
    Your Man. 30
Your Feminine Voice: 32
You're Not Outback Steakhouse—Don't Accept Last-
    Minute Reservations: 33
Dear Ms. Avi - Business Cards 35

**Chapter 3—Where to Meet a Mensch and Other
Awkward Party Situations** 37
A Glossary Before We Go Hunting: 37
Jewish Events: 39
Mensch-Friendly Non-Specifically Jewish Events: 43

A Word on Numbers: 47
Be the New Girl in Town—Even if You've Been Here
    Five Years: 48
Work on Your Jew-dar: 49
Dear Ms. Avi - Jewish Events? 51

Chapter 4—Online, Speed-Dating, and Set-Ups: Toto,
   We're Not in the Old Country Anymore 52
Date Like a Shiksa in Cyberspace: 53
On Which Sites Can You Buy Kosher Beef? 53
The Perfect Pictures that Get You Free Meals: 55
Let's Write a Bunch of Lies, Shall We?: 56
Reading, Responding, and the Shiksa Shabbat: 57
First Encounters of the Jewish Male Kind: 58
Facebook, LinkedIn, and Other Stalking Mechanisms: 61
Speed-Dating 101: 62
What to Wear to Speed-Dating: 63
Hire a Wing-Jew for the Night: 64
After the Awkwardness Ends: 64
Set-ups—The Other White Mitzvah: 65
How to Be Set Up: 65
Step-by-Step Instructions on How to Perform a Set-Up: ... 66
Dear Ms. Avi - When to Remove Profile 68

Chapter 5—Date Like a Shiksa. 69
How to Handle the "Where Should We Meet?" Dilemma: . 69
Wait, When, Where: You're Picking Me Up Saturday
    at 6:00, Right? 71
Acting Like a Shiksa: 72
Leave the JAP at Home: 72
Play the Dumb Blonde Card…Smartly: 73
The Shiksa Compliment: 74
Let the Insecure Jewish Boy Shine: 75
Positive and Happy, Even if You're Not: 75
And When the Check Comes 76
Leave Him Wanting More: 77
"Are You Going to Call Me? *Please?*" 77

Lanny, and Tommy, and Brett, Oh My!. 78
WTF Are We?. 79
No Answer Is Your Answer:. 80
Dear Ms. Avi - How to Use a Phone 82

**Chapter 6—Let Him Define the Relationship (Or at
Least Let Him Believe That):** 84
Pace the Relationship Like a Shiksa: 84
Men May Love Bitches, But Eventually He'll Want to
See Your Nurturing Side: 85
Jewish Friendography and How to Not Be a Clinger: 86
No Need to Buy His Affection—The Shiksa Gift: 87
Mishpucha and the Two Jewish Mothers: 88
"Dude…You're So Whipped": 91
How Much Crap Should I Leave at His Place?: 91
Moving in and Hosting Shabbat Dinner Every Friday
Night Together: 91

**Chapter 7—Be the Preacher's Daughter: Sex, Sin, and
Recognizing the Kosher Player** 94
A Change in Definition: 95
Hold Off as Long as You Can:. 96
The Green Signal: 98
Sexy Time Kosher Style Q&A: 99
Dear Ms. Avi - Hooking Up 102

**Chapter 8—Evaluate Like the Shiksa: Is He Actually
your Prince Mensching?** 104
Ms. Avi's List of Factors That Matter: 105
Time to Part Like the Red Sea? 108
Your Eggs, Wasting Time, and Vasectomies: 108
If He Calls It Quits: 110
If You De-Mensched: 112
Dear Ms. Avi - How to Dump 113

Concluding Thoughts:. 115

Selected Bibliography and Recommended Reading. 119

Acknowledgements:

An especially big thank-you to Jodi, my editor, for helping me turn this rough around the edges guide into a semi-legit book that sometimes uses English grammar. Thank you to Lori who provided me with the initial guidance and confidence that I could make this work.

To all of the people I got to bug with questions on a regular basis: Miriam, Stacy (my PR rep), Julie, Melissa (my go-to shiksa), Vicki, Ivan, Barry, John, Rachel, S. Party, Karen, Jennifer, Jillian, Heather, and Laura. Cousin Jordy, I know you tried to read it, but were in Russia, but you mentioned me in your bat-mitzvah speech, so I figured I'd mention you here.

This book was inspired by Ellen Fein and Sherrie Schneider, best-selling authors of *The Rules*. If you have not read their book, I would highly recommend it. Ellen and Sherrie also gave me the advice to not ever dare mention to my boyfriend that I was writing a dating book. Let's see how that works out...

Thank you to Samuel Kanner for the hand-drawn cover design that happens to not resemble me in the slightest. She is a looker though...

To my parents and sister, thanks for hopefully speaking with me again after this gets published. I've printed out a special copy just for you that doesn't include Chapter 7.

To all of you who have purchased this book, criticized it, recommended it to friends, and liked it on Facebook, I appreciate it.

Introduction

I once drove a boyfriend into the arms of a shiksa. The following pages are my attempt to make up for that:

His name was Adam. He cared about his faith and wanted to pass on more about Judaism than just bagels to his future unborn-lawyer offspring. Unfortunately I tried to change the way he dressed, was a bit of a clinger, and left him with a sour taste in his mouth for Jewish women. The next year, I learned the hard way—through Facebook—that he had a new girlfriend named Catherine O'Malley. With the shiksiest of all shiksa names, it was highly doubtful that she was a tribesmate. Not that I had anything against her; I'm sure she came from a lovely family. But I couldn't stop my pretty little finger from clicking through their twenty Facebook pictures together—it was like not being able to look away from a train wreck. There was the evidence before me—one photo of them at the beach, one of them sipping eggnog at her family Christmas party, and one of them making out on New Year's Eve. I would not have been jealous if he were dating a Rebecca or a Shira, but a Catherine? According to a Talmudic saying, when you save a life, you save the whole world. Should I be held responsible for the destruction of the Jewish tradition because I treated an ex-boyfriend poorly and drove a former Hebrew School all-star into the arms of a Catholic girl?

There's a lot I would have done differently had I known then what I know now about shiksa appeal and attracting quality Jewish men. Some naïve Jewish women solely blame shiksas for our men straying and ask, "How do we counteract them? And more importantly, how do we remove their profiles from JDate?" We can either bitch about shiksas stealing our men or we can *learn from them* and prevent them from doing that in the first place! We Jewish women have so many admirable qualities, but there is room for improvement. In this book, we'll delve into the looks and behaviors that most Jewish men are looking for in a woman. We'll also reveal what makes shiksas so attractive to Jewish men, and how you, too, can emulate them without losing your unique identity.

Why Write About *Them*?

In case you are not familiar with the term, shiksa, a Yiddish word meaning "blemish," describes a non-Jewish woman. The context is usually derogatory, because only a little more than half of American Jews marry within the faith. Of those who intermarry, only one-third end up raising their children Jewish. Some Orthodox Jews go so far as to call intermarriage the *Silent Holocaust.* But are our men entirely to blame? If you were a slightly socially awkward Jewish male, wouldn't that All-American girl-next door in your biochem class tempt you? Wouldn't you want her touching your matzo balls, too?

Believe it or not, shiksas have existed just as long as Jews have—yet we still overcame for all this time! First they were multi-god-worshipping Pagans. Then they morphed into cute blonde Catholic girls, and now they're also petite Asian girls in med school. But so far, the Jews have survived and procreated anyway.

Our challenges today differ from those of the past. We can no longer rely on the insular shtetl life or alienation from the rest of society to ensure Jewish procreation. We no longer wear yellow stars, nor are we all living in the densely populated Lower East Side of Manhattan. Despite the hardships of tenement life, it was significantly easier to find your kosher beef when your neighbors and classmates were all Jewish!

When our great-grandparents walked off that one-star cruise ship from Eastern Europe, their goal was to be American—and some lost their Judaism along the way. Today we are accepted members of society, without the shtetls, ghettos, or the Pale of Settlement that kept us separated from (yet intertwined with) the outside world. The price we pay for religious freedom in America is that:

1. Our children are surrounded by and befriended by non-Jews in school and in their communities.
2. We no longer impose strict consequences (such as excommunication from a family) by dating or marrying outside the faith. Back in the old country (and still among religious circles), families sit shiva for a child who marries a goy. Today, intermarriage is such a common occurrence that secular Jewish mothers embrace their Gentile daughters-in-law or they risk driving their children away from the family.

Furthermore, our multicultural society encourages diversity and intermingling among races and discourages different sections of society from remaining separated. I'm not going to lie; as much as I love my fried rice, I realize that enjoying fattening Chinese foods comes at a price, not only for my midline but also because it lessens family pressure to marry within the faith. Our cushy lifestyle, filled with diversity and other big words, has unfortunately relieved the pressure to marry into bagels and lox. Jewish education (for the majority of American Reform and Conservative Jews) ends at age thirteen once the bar-mitzvah checks are cashed. Because of this, many young Jews do not stay connected to the community. It's pretty obvious why almost half of American Jews don't marry under the Chuppah.

A mother's best defense against her nice Jewish son going for the Lucy Liu look-alike is to raise her son with a strong Jewish education, a love of their heritage and culture, and strong Jewish values. Studies have shown that the more years of religious education a Jewish child receives, the less likely he/she will be to intermarry. As young females, our best defense is to learn from the shiksa (or move to Israel or Borough Park). Oftentimes she's not the problem—we are. Our behavior turns off the nice Jewish boy. We cruelly reject the Jewish males who want us and we act desperate, drunk, and giddy around the ones we'd like to take home to mom. This conduct sends him right into the arms of a shiksa who doesn't nag, complain or whine. She is waiting to get her perfectly-manicured hands on our kosher beef. Unfortunately there are two prevalent stereotypes of Jewish women. *Note: Yes, we deserve and have earned these labels:*

1. The overbearing Jewish mother stereotype—Let me tell my man what to do, when to do it, and how to do it. So sexy.
2. The JAP (Jewish American Princess) label—We chickadees earned this stereotype at age thirteen with our over-the-top bat mitzvahs, our fear of the smallest bug in the woods, and our matching Elsa Paretti necklaces, earrings, and bracelets from Tiffany's.

To take our men back, we Jewish women must look our best, get involved in life outside work, treat potential suitors well even if we are not interested in them, and not wait until age 35 to open up to the idea of marriage. There are so many smart, educated, beautiful, and athletic Jewish women out there who defy the negative stereotypes, and I want them to be able to attract quality men.

But as a woman, your children will automatically be Jewish, so why limit yourself to a fraction of men who represent 2.2% of the US population? I'll be the first to admit, there are some bizarre, socially awkward, and hobbit-like Jewish men out there who you'd swear were extras in *Lord of the Rings*. At the 2005 Matzo Ball in New York City, there was even a 4'7" man in a tuxedo dancing alone in the middle of the dance floor. And to say that these bizarre creatures are a small minority within the active Jewish population would be nothing but a lie.

However, despite these seemingly adverse odds, Jewish men really do make wonderful husbands and fathers. Besides the fact that they share a heritage with you, they also are generally good providers, faithful, dependable, well-educated, and love children. Don't tell anyone, but I'm a sucker for a Yid with a good resume. By marrying within the faith, you're also keeping a 4,000 year old tradition alive while preventing Great-Grandma from turning in her grave. As Leah Furman so eloquently states in her book *Single Jewish Female*, "Every time you go on a date or start a relationship with a non-Jew, you shut out opportunities to meet a perfectly suitable Jewish guy."

Some Basic Truths:
Before we dive into the wonderful world of kosher dating and shiksa appeal, there are a few dating truths we should discuss:

Truth #1: Okay, you didn't hear it from me, but ... not all Jewish guys go to temple on Friday night. In fact, usually the more successful, good-looking ones do not. In a melting-pot society, it's inevitable that some Jewish men are going to date the shiksa next door instead of the nice Jewish girl at shul. When it comes to dating, there are three basic categories of Jewish men:

1. Guys who don't want to date Jewish women. Most of these men had bad experiences with Jappy girls in their childhood and hold on to negative stereotypes that are absolutely not true for all women.
2. Guys who are open to dating Jewish women, but don't specifically seek us out. Oftentimes, these men consider it a *bonus* if a girl is Jewish, but don't rule out women solely based on their religion.
3. Guys who only date Jewish women either because they love us Jewish chicks or because marrying Jewish is important to them.

The focus of this book is to reel in men from categories 2 and 3. Forget about the self-hating Jews that fall into category 1. One extreme personal story involves a guy I knew who accepted a set-up with a girl, but then found out she was a quarter Jewish, and he was suddenly no longer interested. Avoid some of the negative stereotypes and you'll find more and more boys in yarmulkes winking at you, not only on JDate, but in real life too!

Truth #2: When a man meets you, the little bar mitzvah boy in his pants either likes what it sees or doesn't. End of story. Only bother with men who are into you, and who pursue you. Then decide how you feel about them, not the other way around. It is counter-productive to waste time thinking about (or God forbid, chasing after) guys who do not notice you or are not attracted to you. "Love only those who love you," as Sherrie Schneider and Ellen Fein of *The Rules* say. These simple words should guide you in your romantic relationships and keep you from obsessing over men who are not interested in you. The moral of this near-biblical-in-proportions story is: let the guys who are naturally attracted to you come toward you.

Why Chasing After Guys Who Don't Like You Is Ridiculous:

✡ You waste time.

✡ You inflate his already huge ego.

✡ The man who eventually chases and gets you is the lucky one.

✡ You look like a fool when you profess your love to him or chase him.

✡ You give yourself false hope, which leads to …

   ○ Getting taken advantage of.

   ○ Joining activities you're not interested in because he does them.

   ○ Waiting around his local coffee shop for hours waiting for him to walk in, sit next to you, and ask you out.

✡ You end up agonizing over how he feels about you.

✡ Since he's a guy, he's probably willing to hook up with you. If you do hook up, you'll convince yourself that he has feelings for you, but in reality he only has feelings for feeling you up.

✡ If you're attempting to become friends with him, you will end up heartbroken when he finds a girlfriend who is not you (but hopefully, she'll at least be Jewish).

Truth #3: Men are biologically programmed to want someone who looks nice and will make nice-looking babies. Women want providers, someone who will make them feel safe and will be able to support their future family and pay for their son's bar mitzvah. So what does this mean? You need to look nice and allow him to provide for you. If he doesn't treat you well on a date, he's not worth your time.

7

Yes, I hate to admit it, but your looks are your first few meal tickets for nice dates. After that, he will care about your personality. Let him take care of you and be the provider on the date. He's looking for a feeling that he's "needed" to provide, even if you have your own paycheck and car. There are many ways to make him feel needed. Let him pay, pick out the first few dates, and be the aggressor sexually. Just make sure to appreciate everything he provides for you. Exhibiting a sense of entitlement and acting like a JAP will turn any man off and have him running for the nearest small-town shiksa who appreciates everything he offers.

> Some Jewish women are in denial, or, as The Situation (from *The Jersey Shore*) would say, they are "haters." These haters think, "Oh, I can throw myself at whoever I want." Or these women might say, "I don't want a man who likes me for my looks." Well, honeybuns, it's not that a man doesn't care that you're successful. It's that unless you look good, your success doesn't really matter to him. A hater needs to change her attitude immediately, or she will be waiting a long time to find a man who is willing to date her.

Truth #4: A man's biological clock starts ticking when he hits forty—or at thirty if he's balding and/or a little tubby. Whenever it starts, he knows his promiscuous days are coming to a dreary end; it's time to hit the singles events and find a fertile woman to impregnate while he still has slightly more sex appeal than Harry Goldenblatt. (Isn't he darling?) Jewish male-pattern balding is actually the great equalizer for the Jewish woman. Without it, our men would all be playboys until fifty! Evaluate your man as you would a sale at Loehmann's; if you don't buy the DKNY dress today, a shiksa might take if off the rack tomorrow. And don't hang around too long if there's no chance of a ring! Your eggs aren't getting any younger.

Truth #5: At times, it's great to be single. At other times, it's not so great. But the fact of the matter is that you have to be single to find your future partner—unless, of course, you're open to cheating (and as tempting as that sounds, someday he'll wake up and ask himself, "She cheated on the ex; would she cheat on me?"). As a (gasp) "single," you're sometimes lonely, bored, and a little "on edge." You show up at the Passover Seder at Aunt Verna's house with your parents, and everyone says, "But she's so nice; she must have intimacy problems." But staying with someone who treats you poorly only worsens your chances of finding your *beshert*.

This is not to say that you should rush from relationship to relationship and attach yourself to the first live guy who asks you on a date. Being single (and maybe even having a little fun) is an essential step towards finding the one. See below for the good sides of single-hood:

Just for Kicks—Ms. Avi's List of Good Things About Being Single:

✡ You can go to events, parties, and bars and give out your number like candy on Halloween (only to guys who ask for it, of course).

✡ Dating is fun because you get ...

    ○ Free meals

    ○ Dating stories that end up as good stories for your book on shiksa appeal (whoops)

✡ You have plenty of time for your female friends.

Ok, that's all I can think of. So let's help you get out and find a boyfriend!

What You Will Learn: The 8-Step Method:

Now that we know what we're dealing with, how are you going to reel him in? Here is a sneak-peak of what's to be covered in the following eight chapters. For best results, add your own spice to fit the plan to your unique character and lifestyle:

1. **Shiksify Your Look:** This first chapter emphasizes the importance of your appearance. In order to attract quality men (and keep them drooling over you till your grandkids' weddings), you must put as much effort into your appearance as any God-fearing shiksa would. If that means buying a new dress for Shabbat that goes a little above your knees—then so be it! Since you're not a lesbian, don't rely on the opinions of your girlfriends; ask your male friends what they find sexy, and wear that.

2. **Playing Hard to Get, Shiksa Style:** In this chapter, we'll explore how Jewish men love to be challenged and made to feel masculine. Let him sweat a little by playing it cool. A shiksa would never ramble on out of nervousness just because she is speaking with a kosher beefcake, and neither should you!

3. **Where to Meet a Mensch and Other Awkward Party Situations:** Go where the Jewish boys are! They're not hiding under your couch, so go to events (Jewish *and* non-specifically Jewish events). You'll find eligible men out in the open at Jewish events, but many are hiding in sports leagues, sports bars, night clubs, political groups, outdoors groups, or political campaigns.

4. **Online, Speed-Dating, and Set-ups—Toto, We're not in the Shtetl Anymore:** Have no shame; use these valuable resources to your full advantage. Your Great-Great-Grandmother in the old country had five eligible men in

her shtetl, so the town yenta fixed her up with the balding ones who were twenty years her senior. Do it for great- great-grandma; she'd want you to use these tools.

5. **Date Like a Shiksa:** Once you've met an eligible man who's asked you out, act gracious and confident on the date, as any shiksa would. Take into account all that you learned in Chapter 2, and knock his socks off with your mysteriousness, confidence, and radiance.

6. **Let Him Define the Relationship (Or at Least Let him Believe That):** Follow the advice in this chapter to keep him once you've caught him. Pace the relationship so he doesn't flee in the opposite direction!

7. **Be the Preacher's Daughter—Sex, Sin, and Recognizing the Kosher Player:** Make Ms. Avi proud and say, "Yes" to a nice free meal and, "No, thank you" to unmeaningful physical encounters. Learn how to spot and avoid the men who just want to play you so that you don't waste your time on one.

8. **Evaluate Like the Shiksa—Is He Actually Your Prince Mensching?:** Recognize whether a man is trying to get in your pants or to get a very expensive ring on your finger. Hopefully, it's the latter of the two. Recognize if he's "the one," and move on if he's not. If you dump him, be sure to dump him with class; you don't want him hating all nice Jewish girls!

Have Faith in Our Kind:

Although you should observe the shiksas and take notes, the last thing you want to do is give up your Jewishness, dye your hair blonde, and become one of them. If you really wanted to be a shiksa, you could easily accept Jesus Christ as your savior and you'd have two billion new friends welcoming you. But why do that? We

Jewish chicks have some great qualities, such as brains, beauty, big boobs, intellectual passion, warmth, family values, good "oral communication" skills, and humor. We're told that Jewish girls act a certain way, and that Jewish men don't want us. Don't believe it. Know that Jewish men *and* non-Jewish men find you attractive. It's true. Just look around JDate; you'll spot a few guys named Tyrone looking to get their hands all over us. We are indeed in demand! The key is to embrace the positive Jewish qualities and defy the negative stereotypes. I strive to make all Jewish chickadees irresistible to their kosher counterparts. My dream is for Gentile males to wish they were Jewish so they, too, could snuggle with hot Jewish women!

There was once a time without JDate, speed-dating, and Christmas Eve matzo ball parties, and Jews managed to find each other and procreate anyway. If you're looking and feeling your best, men will find you attractive. Get out there. Bitter Betties don't find boyfriends—they keep cats, instead. Meeting new men (not the same men over and over again, but new men) is a key to success. Eventually you will meet the right one. By the end of this book, you may want to send me hate mail or you may see the world of dating in a whole new light. Hopefully the latter.

Please keep in mind that this is not a guide for how to use shiksa appeal to find a hook up … or a f*ck buddy or anything else they're called these days. Anyone (who lowers her standards enough) can get sex. Go to a party, and try that heavy guy next to the bowl of Cheetos who's been eyeing you all night. I'm sure he's up for it. But you're looking for more—a loving relationship with a man who treats you with respect—you should not be willing to degrade yourself in the process of finding love.

The 8-Step Ms. Avi Method is about believing that you're beautiful and that a wonderful man who loves you will come along one day. This no-BS guide will help you work through the issues that plague Jewish women in today's changing dating world and hopefully help you find your shul-mate. I wish you loads of luck on your journey. So let's work together, gain some shiksa characteristics, embrace our Jewishness, and prevent the kidnapping of yet another Jewish man by an innocent-looking Catholic woman.

Enjoy!

Dear Ms. Avi,
You talk a lot about men dating outside of Judaism, but what about women?

Regards, Shana

Dear Shana,

To solely focus on men marrying shiksas would only be half the story. According to author Christine Benvenuto, "Even now, when Jewish women have begun 'marrying out' in numbers comparable to their brothers, popular belief has it that their change of heart owes as much to pragmatism as preference: there simply aren't enough Jewish men to go around." So if marrying a goy is because of numbers as opposed to choice, at what point do we throw in the towel, give up on finding our very own Jeff Goldblum? (aka, the sexiest man of the mid-nineties!) When should I consider dating outside of the religion?

Ms. Avi encourages you to only date Jewish men, but there's one exception. If you find yourself in the position of being over 35 and single, it is probably worth your while to expand your dating pool to include sheygetzim (male shiksas). This is the exception.

Ms. Avi's Reasons Why it's Okey-Dokey to Expand the Pool After 35:
✡ If you plan on having children with a man, it's best to be married before 40. Sure there are stories of women who give birth at 50, but those are the exception, not the rule.
✡ Your children will be Jewish because you're Jewish.
✡ A Gentile man is better than no man at all.

Just to clarify, this only applies to women. There is no biological reason for a man to expand his dating pool just because he's hit 35. Love always, Ms. Avi

Chapter 1—

Shiksify Your Look:
Be Yourself, Just Better

Not every Jewish girl can have naturally blonde hair, but all Jewish girls can morph into the shiksa goddess he's not supposed to date. He'll feel badass because he's dating you, but yet his family will approve—and he'll love it! All you need to do is shiksify your look...

So how do you go about shiksifying your look? The first step is to think about what your mother looks like—and try to look nothing like her. Even if she's a looker like Bette Midler, she is still a Jewish mother, and therefore you want to be nothing like her (unless she is a convert, and then she *really* knows her shiksa appeal). Most guys would rather date Susan Boyle than date someone who looks or acts like their mother. Even if the Jewish girl has the same face, body, and hair type as his mother, if she acts differently and dresses differently, then he will not perceive her to be like the woman whose uterus he spent nine months in.

I know, I know—all Jewish women will eventually turn into Jewish mothers. The trick is to prevent him from seeing you in that light. Although this chapter is about looks, it extends beyond the superficial. You need to dress and act like the shiksa vixen he wants to be with, but shouldn't. She knows how to attract a man, not mother a man. Oh, and don't forget Bubbe. Avoid mimicking her, too. As much as everyone loves Bubbe, she's not attracting the hotties like she used to with her blinged-out Juicy Couture purple sweat suit. She's in Fort Lauderdale, where the ratio of women to men in her retirement community is six to one.

This chapter isn't first because I'm shallow, nor is it first because men are shallow. Men are *visual*, not shallow … and this gives them the appearance of shallowness. And as long as you accept this fact, you are on the path to success with men.✿ If this book is a menorah, then looking good is the Shamash, the tallest candle. The Shamash is the first candle lit, and it is used to light all the other candles on the menorah. You don't have confidence without looking good, and you don't get dates without looking good (unless, of course, your JDate picture looks good).

You *Are Sexy!*

Looking your best means being a confident woman above all else. Don't let those magazines, filled with girls who haven't eaten anything more than a matzo ball all year tell you otherwise. Men find all shapes, hair colors, and eye colors sexy. Stand up straight, push your shoulders back, and walk into a room with confidence and a smile.

Okay, now that we're friends and have gone through the mushy BS section, it's time to be frank. So you have two options:

✿ Women who do not put effort into their appearance and expect men to like them anyway are also *haters*.

1. Be unkempt and bitter, and say, "Oh, I'm gonna find a great guy who's not shallow and sees my inner beauty." Good luck, honey.
2. Accept that men are visual and that there are certain steps you can take to entice that well-educated, sweet, and attractive Jewish male.

To do this, you need to put effort into your appearance, put on some heels, dress for men, and put yourself out there!

That's Nice, Ms. Avi, But...

All of us were given looks by God. Some are more fortunate than others in certain departments. I was given a slow metabolism and a large Jewish nose, but muscular legs and blonde hair (slightly enhanced by highlights). What I'm trying to say is that the majority of us have physical strengths and flaws. I recognize that I have nice legs, so I primarily wear shirts that cover my arms, and instead choose to show off my legs. As opposed to kvetching about your physical disadvantages, you can mask them and highlight other beautiful features (or change them through plastic surgery). Knowing what males find attractive is the key to bringing out your best attributes and looking like that shiksa he's not supposed to date. Yentl, get ready to kill them with your looks.

A Grand List of What Men Find Attractive About Women:

✡ Boobs of any kind—Men find *all* boobs sexy, but especially big ones, and lucky for us, there's a stereotype that Jewish women are large on top. Men don't have to know if they sag; that's what bras are for. Your bra is your friend. Make friends with one who lifts you up, and doesn't let you fall down. Remember, he only finds out how saggy you are once the lights go down and the clothes come off, and if you follow my rules, by then he will like your personality and saggy boobs won't be a deal-breaker.

✡ Not too much junk in the trunk—Thin wins in the dating world. I'm a huge supporter of Weight Watchers because it's a lifestyle, not a yo-yo diet. I cannot tell you how many more men will ask you out when you're less "fluffy." Find an eating/exercise plan that works for you, and stick with it long-term. Shiksas don't yo-yo diet; they stay at a healthy weight.

✡ Legs—Unless you have a massive scar that extends from your buttocks to your knee, you probably have nice legs. Let them out to play.

✡ No lesbian hairdos—Even if you think you look better and more stylish with short hair, most guys prefer you with long, feminine hair. The ability to grow long hair is a sign you have been in good health for a number of years and tells your future mother-in-law that you are ready to bear her grandchildren. But cut it off when you look like a ragamuffin or a seventy- year-old hippie!

✡ Curly vs. Straight—A debate as fundamental as latke vs. hamantaschen. This can be quite the sore subject for Jewish women. Despite popular belief, many men do go for curly, "Jewish," hair. If you've evaluated your curly locks and noticed that they look better straight, then don't be ashamed to embrace your inner shiksa and straighten your hair. Our kind also seems to have a nack for acquiring frizzy hair (maybe it was from all those years wandering around the desert). This is a major no-no for any God-fearing shiksa, so if you were the unlucky recipient of frizzy hair, buy some product and a flat-iron.

✡ A pearly-white smile—Few quick fixes are as dramatic as getting your teeth whitened.

✡ Clear skin—Okay, pizza face, if you're over seventeen, it's time to get rid of the acne. The clearer your skin, the less cover-up you'll need. Get chemical peels, microdermabrasion, antibiotics, the pill, or laser treatment. You may even want to inquire with your dermatologist to see if there are treatments your insurance will cover. Why does insurance cover chemical peels? I have no idea, but you may as well take advantage of it if you can.

Shiksas Don't Wear Schmatas!

My mother once told me that, "Women dress to impress other women." I pondered over this and thought, "Hell, no." If you're dressing for other women, you better be a lesbian and looking for a lady. Otherwise, you're just wasting your time. If you're straight (and just happened to make out with your girlfriend once when you were drunk), then get your goals in line and start dressing like a shiksa would, according to what men find appealing. Ask yourself what looks good on your body, and wear the clothes that hide your flaws instead of accentuating them. (Capped sleeves are nobody's friend.) Men are simple; we all know what they find appealing, and not much has changed in the past fifty years. For some extra advice on how to dress to attract, read below:

✡ Confidence and a smile—Confidence and a smile always make you look beautiful and more approachable! No slouching.

✡ Feminine clothes—Men are attracted to women. Nowadays, if they wanted to date men, they would; it's called homosexuality. But hopefully, you want to attract a heterosexual male, so dress like a lady. This seemingly obvious statement will hopefully coerce you to take off those baggy jeans and put on a pair that shows your well-toned tuchas.

✡ Wear an outfit that shows off your shape—This is not necessarily the most revealing outfit, but something that shows off your waist or legs. Let them use their imaginations to visualize what's underneath. (Their minds will take ten pounds off your body!) Because you are Jewish, there is a high chance that you have good baby-bearing hips. Wear clothes that accentuate your waist-to-hip ratio, such as a wrap dress.

✡ Add some color—Black may be the easy way out, but if you really want a man to notice and remember you, add some color to your wardrobe. A bold or brightly-colored shirt or dress will always grab his attention—every good shiksa knows this.

✡ Heels—No matter if they cost $20 or $200—men won't know the difference and don't care—they just love heels. Heels make your legs look longer and your whole body look thinner, define the muscles, and make your bum sway from side to side. They are also sexy from a biological standpoint because only fit/healthy women wear heels. There are exceptions to when you should wear heels, and we'll discuss them later in the chapter.

✡ Necklines—Tank tops, V-necks, and scoop necks that show off the bottom of the neck and/or shoulders are fabulous because they remind men that you have a chest without showing *too* much cleavage. A bit of cleavage is great because it's a signal to men that you are approachable and came dressed to attract their attention.

✡ Hike it up, baby—Wear shorts, skirts, dresses, hot pants, and sequined unitards—anything that shows off your legs.

✡ Makeup—Jewish girls, especially in Los Angeles, are known for conspicuously slathering on too much make-up. The shiksa uses foundation to make her skin look polished. She gives off the impression that her skin is naturally flawless. Mascara and a little eyeliner go a long way to making your eyes look bigger. You can never wear too much mascara, unless it's caked on so heavily that it causes your eyelashes to fall out. Eyeliner, on the other hand, is a different story. If you wear too much, it looks like you're either trying too hard or are a five-dollar hooker. Last, the lips are not to be forgotten.

Appropriateness Is Sexy:

Although you want to make sure to attract, you also don't want to attract negative attention based on your outfit in the wrong venue. We've all seen the girl who shows up at the professional event with the skirt that nips right below the bum. It screams desperation. The shiksa knows that dressing appropriate for the situation is sexy. So be sure to hike it up, but just not *too* high.

Look Cute in Unsuspecting Places:

As important as it is to get out there and meet eligible men, it's equally essential that you make sure you look your best when you do. When you're at a bar or party, everyone is sluttily dressed and has their A-game on. Well, everyone looks good when the lights are dim, even the fuglies. Here's Ms. Avi's secret trick—look extra cute in unsuspecting places. You may recall from your college days (or last night if you are still in college) that the trend is to look unkempt on every occasion except when going out to get trashed. My friend, Sasha, was the exception. She had this down to a science. During club soccer practices, where she knew the competition was unsuspecting, she brought her A-game. She wore sexy athletic wear and natural-looking makeup to play soccer. She made sure to show off her legs and to act womanly and graceful on the field.

She ended up marrying a doctor she met at soccer who might not have noticed her if he'd just met her at a frat party where all the girls looked hot.

Just as you want to meet men who are gainfully employed, men want to meet attractive women. Men want women who not only look scrumptious on Saturday night, but who also look good cleaning the house. Looking good in unsuspecting places, however, does not mean showing up to Shabbat services in a prom dress. Keep in mind, there is a fine line between looking naturally cute and looking ridiculously made up.

What to Wear on a Date:

If he asked you out, it's a fact that he already finds you physically attractive—unless, of course, your mothers set you up on a date and he was guilted into going out with you. Keep up that sexy image by wearing an outfit on your date that screams class and sex appeal all at the same time. This is achieved by following the rule of "Shiksa Sexy, not Slutty" by showing off one body part at a time, such as the legs, arms, or slight cleavage—just not the whole enchilada at once! Even if you choose to dress modestly, it can be made sexy, as long as the shape of your body is evident. The keys for dressing for a date are to look hot without trying too hard as well as dress appropriately for the venue/activity.

Ms. Avi's Guide to What to Wear Where:
Nine out of ten men surveyed agree that a dress is the hottest and most feminine clothing item a woman can wear on a date. So wear one if you can!
Note: If you are taller than him, then skip the heels and see page 25.

If you're going on a:

✡ Bar Date: Hot, informal dress to show off legs with heels.

✡ Romantic Dinner: Appropriate dress for the venue with heels, or jeans and sexy shirt, and be sure to show off one body part.

✡ Coffee/Lunch Date: Jeans, shorts, or informal dress and flats. (You can wear heels if wearing jeans).

✡ Ice Skating Adventure: Jeans with a cute sweater.

✡ Movie and Make-out Date: Jeans, hot shirt, and heels.

✡ Mini-Golfing Date: Cute shorts or jeans, shirt with flats (or else your heel will get stuck in the hole, and you will fall flat on your face—not very shiksa-esque).

✡ Boring Museum Date: Informal dress (with flats) or jeans (with heels) and cute shirt.

✡ Tennis Date: Sexy shorts and shirt or tennis skirt (if you have the skills to back it up).

✡ Pro-Sports Game: Jeans and a hot shirt, heels if night, flats if day.

✡ Speed-Dating: Dress or brightly colored shirt/jeans (men will remember you better in color), heels. If it's a Friday or Saturday night, wear a dress.

Now that you look the part of that hot shiksa that any man would open up his wallet for, it's time to act the part. At some point you have to open your mouth, so read on about how to wow him with your mysterious shiksa personality (with maybe a little manipulation thrown in for good measure). Once you've mastered these skills, you'll unlock the door to let the male attention flood in.

Dear Ms. Avi,

I get that heels are hot. I get that they make my legs look longer and me thinner. But let's face the facts, I'm 5'10", and half the Jewish guys I meet come up to my chin. Why are Jewish men not allowed to be taller than 5'8"? Do I still wear heels?

Best,
Rachel

Dear Rachel,
If you are taller than your date, you should wear flats at first to bring out his masculinity (and to not rub it in his face that he is vertically challenged.) But men sometimes dig chicks who are taller than they are, such as the happily divorced couple Tom Cruise and Nicole Kidman. Some short guys will even tell you to wear heels anyway (because they make your legs look so scrumptious), and you just need to put on your detectives hat to determine his preference. But play it safe for at least the first few dates and wear flats.

Much love,
Ms. Avi

Chapter 2-

Playing Hard to Get, Shiksa Style

The good Christian girl is an enigma to our men. She comes from an exotic culture that includes Easter ham and she isn't impressed by the fact that a man's last name ends in "berg." She is not awe-struck by the hot male (usually scrawny) kosherness. As a result, Jewish men do view shiksas as more challenging than us. As Maurice Berger finds in *The Mouse that Never Roars: Jewish Masculinity on American Television*, "His love interest is most often cool and critical; she [the shiksa] demands respect and often makes her partner beg for her affection." How can the shiksa afford to be so aloof? Well, these women have no pressure to marry Jewish from their parents. Also, they also come from non-Jewish households and cultures, so they're mysterious and harder to understand.

Well, we may not be able to become the "other" like the shiksa is, but we absolutely can pick up some pointers from her when it comes to challenging men. The next few pages will cover playing hard to get by maintaining composure, using your feminine voice, allowing men to chase after you, learning to receive, and not accepting last minute invitations. These principles will have you on your way to becoming that aloof shiksa who attracts men like flies to a bug-zapper.

You're Jewish Too? Great, I'm Gonna Throw Myself at You:

It's clear that we're playing a numbers game. Every time a Jewish man dates a goy, there are fewer fish with fins and scales left for us Jewish girls in the dating pool. So how does our kind react? With a limited supply of kosher fish in the sea, when we meet one, we might think, "Oh my God, you're Jewish too, will you marry me?" and start acting giddy and borderline desperate. Your heart may be racing, but don't let him know that, or you risk stroking his ego. Instead, make yourself mysterious and challenging like a shiksa, and don't act dazzled by him.

When you act nervous around a guy, it lowers your value. What goes through his mind is: "Hey, this girl likes me; she must be easy to get with and/or a loser." Remember, it was the pretty cheerleaders who had the hot boyfriends in high school. Carry yourself as if you were the hot cheerleader in high school, and the boys will believe it.

Respect yourself enough to know that men will ask you out, and that if you make yourself easy, a man may get with you, but will not stay with you. Many Jewish men are well aware that their Jewishness makes them more attractive in our eyes. A shiksa wouldn't be fazed by the fact that he's Jewish, and neither should you. Allow him to appreciate the wonders of being with a woman who shares a common heritage and who is still sexy and challenging.

Through my many interviews with men, I learned that one of the most interesting reasons men are attracted to shiksas is the lack of pressure on the relationship. When he meets a Jewish woman, the pressure is on. When he meets a shiksa, he opens up oftentimes because he thinks in his mind that the relationship cannot go anywhere. Then one thing leads to another and he ends up with her phone number, and then the phone number leads to a date. By removing the pressure when you meet a Jewish man by playing it cool and not mentioning marriage or the future, you let him relax and really get to know you as a person.

Study Her:

You may be asking, "But Ms. Avi, how can I make myself more challenging or interesting?" The secret to making yourself challenging is to treat the hottest guy you know no differently from how you treat that guy you have zero interest in dating. Shiksas are masters at this. They see a good-looking Jewish guy, and they are not fazed just because he's Jewish. They treat him as if he were a regular guy, because to them he IS a regular guy. (They also don't have the voices of their mothers in the back of their head saying, "When am I getting grandchildren?"). They hold composure when conversing with attractive men. If there's a hot guy in the cube down the hall, the key is to talk to him as if he's nothing special—act as if you have tons of hot guys talking to you all the time.

Maintaining composure doesn't mean being a bore. Show your sassy personality and be sure to laugh once in a while.

You share a religion, heritage, and lactose intolerance with him, but how can you make yourself more seem exotic or "different" to him like the shiksa does? How about having an interesting hobby besides shopping that makes you stand out from the rest of the Jewish girls he meets? Who cares if you're even good at it? How about taking up Tae-Kwon-Do, Krav Maga, fly fishing, or golf? What about studying a language in your spare time such as Hebrew, Arabic, or Portuguese? If you have a unique career to begin with, it's already great conversation material. If you're a teacher, social worker, or another typical female profession, then consider using hobbies to enhance conversations with potential dates.

Don't Chase—Let Them Come After You:

Hey, Betty Freidan, I'm well aware that women got the right to vote and that some of us are now doctors, lawyers, and politicians, but women who deny the biological differences between men (the hunters) and women (the hunted) in the dating jungle are just setting themselves up for disappointment. Did I mention that men love to actively pursue, so you ruin the fun for them if you make yourself easy?

When you let the man be the aggressor in the relationship—by chasing you, calling you, paying for meals, traveling to see you—you give him *nachas*. I'm not talking about the lazy guys who want you to travel an hour to meet them for coffee at their local coffee shop, for a "cup of something wonderful." (This is a true story. A straight man once used those words.) I'm talking about men with good intentions who will bring you flowers and pick you up to impress you. With the Internet, Facebook stalking, and text messaging, it is all too easy to get in contact with women these days, so it is your responsibility to keep yourself challenging and playful.

When a man pursues you, you know that he is attracted to you. When he chases you, it's his decision to take you out, and it is his pleasure to pay for you (even to a wallet-conscious Jew!). You're a beautiful prize to be won, not some desperate girl who would do anything for a boyfriend. You won't get strung along in a relationship in which he is unsure how he feels. It was his choice to get involved, so he obviously cherishes you. Sometimes men are wimps, and they will not break up with you because they either are afraid to break your heart or do not want to give up the goodies. They may string you along and waste your time. If you stop chasing men and let them chase you, the ones who would only waste your time will naturally weed themselves out and reveal the ones that are actually worth your time.

Ways to Tell a Guy Likes You:

Women will yap for hours trying to figure out, "what he's thinking," but as we have discussed, men are simple creatures. Going all the way back to kindergarten, there are obvious signs that a guy finds you attractive. You have reason for suspicion if he:

✡ Moves to sit by you at an event. He may even fight out other guys to sit by you!

✡ Calls you.

✡ E-mails you for no reason.

✡ Invites you out with his friends and they already know who you are because he's been talking about you.

✡ Is always around you.

✡ Is willing to drive thirty minutes just to have coffee with you.

✡ Is happy to give you rides in his car.

✡ Makes plans ahead of time.

✡ Goes to events you plan or goes places he thinks you'll be.

✡ Doesn't ask for the few bucks back for a cab ride or gas.

Learn to Receive—Ask Not What You Can Do for Your Man...

Some of us cook for our men regularly, buy them expensive gifts, and drop everything we're doing because they want to see us. Many women are natural givers. And that's great—with your friends and family or when you're a mother. But you'll have a better shot at holding onto men if you focus your energy on learning to receive graciously as opposed to worrying about giving. When you start dating a man—drop this giving attitude. When you make yourself challenging, you naturally focus on allowing him to provide, pursue, and win you over versus the other way around. Only once you have received, should you reciprocate.

Signs You Might be Giving Too Much:

✡ You travel to see him before he spends the money or makes the effort to travel to you. It's irrelevant whether it's an hour drive away or a plane ride away.

✡ You clean for him all the time, buy him dinner, and feel like you're not getting enough in return. You're left tired and your work performance suffers.

✡ When you're together, the both of you go on and on discussing his job, his work, his family. It's always about him.

✡ You skip girls night because he wants company. Your friends accuse you of centering your life around a guy.

✡ You're the one usually suggesting to spend time together. You plan everything—including nights out and trips.

✡ When he is in need, you drop everything to come to his aid. When you need something, he is playing basketball with the guys.

If you give too much, you will only be left with resentment toward him if he does not reciprocate in the manner you'd envisioned. This is as true for a man you barely know as it is for a man you've been dating for a year. If you find yourself ever giving too much (more than you're receiving), then cut back, and focus again on receiving graciously. Whoever told girls to bake cookies for their men was full of shit. Let him bake you cookies, and then you can eventually reciprocate. I know this is counterintuitive and may seem crueler than pastrami on white, but it's true!

Your Feminine Voice:

Being challenging means maintaining composure. One of the secrets to maintaining composure around men you wish to date is to utilize your feminine voice. Your feminine voice is how you would speak as a Victoria's Secret Model (not Tyra) who's not intimidated by a smart, good-looking guy. You are not desperate. Finding your feminine voice is a learned skill—and an extremely useful skill to pull out of your toolkit when a cute guy comes along.

How to Find Your Feminine Voice:

Picture Sarah Michelle Gellar in *Cruel Intentions*. Everyone wants her, including her own stepbrother! It's about talking slowly, not rambling, and not conversing loudly or in a super-high-pitched Minnie mouse voice, but instead using a sexy, soft voice.

- ✡ Speak slowly (like talking to grandma).
- ✡ No rambling.
- ✡ Pauses in conversation are okay. They show you're not trying too hard.
- ✡ No chatty Cathy's.
- ✡ Be sure to breathe.

All I can say is practice. Practice alone, practice with girlfriends, and practice on your hot young Rabbi. And just for the record, this does work. You would not believe some of the guys I thought were way too good-looking for me who have asked me out because I wore a smile and was calm, cool, and collected when conversing in my feminine voice.

You're Not Outback Steakhouse—Don't Accept Last-Minute Reservations:

Do you want to be the girl he calls just because he's bored, horny, or hungry on Friday night? Accepting a last-minute offer to see a movie or Taylor Swift in concert is completely un-shiksa-like. You know what? He was going to take some other girl who cancelled on him at the last minute, and your number just happened to be in his phone. By the way, if he has Taylor tickets, you're safe, 'cause he's gay anyway.

Accepting last-minute offers for dates is equivalent to saying, "Well, I guess I'm not special enough for potential suitors to make plans with me ahead of time." You want to be with people who respect your time and company enough to call a few days ahead. You're a busy girl, and if he didn't call you by mid-week for the weekend, then it's his loss. If he really likes you, he will make sure to call you early in the week so some other smooth-talking greased-up Jewish boy from Jersey doesn't get you first. Do you want to be that last-minute girl he calls when the girl he asked out first cancelled on him? Men do that. Ms. Avi was once the other girl. A guy I knew asked my friend Sharon to go see a hockey game. I knew she had said no. The next day he asked me out to the museum. He asked me two days before the date, and I accepted because I had nothing better to do that day. Ms. Avi was that Plan B, and there's no B in "Avi." You never want to be Plan B.

If you are the unfortunate victim of a last-minute invitation (less than three days in advance), don't be a bitch when you politely decline: say, "Oh, I've already made plans. I wish I'd known sooner!" Most guys aren't oblivious, and can often take the hint from the, "I wish." (notice I said "most.") But thinking ahead enough to ask you out in advance means he is thinking of you, buttercup, not that other chick.

Ms. Avi's Guide to How Last-Minute is Last-Minute:

If he asks you out for …

That night—"Oh, I've already made plans. I wish I'd known sooner!"

Tomorrow—"Oh, I've already made plans. I wish I'd known sooner!"

Two days from now—"Oh, I've already made plans. I wish I'd known sooner!"

Three or more days from now—"I'd love to."

Leave your Saturday nights open every week until mid-week. Only after you do not get an offer for a date should you make plans with friends.

In summary, in order to attract like a shiksa, making yourself challenging is key. Let him ask you out. Don't fight him when he picks up the bill (and don't even pretend to take out your wallet or do "the reach" if it's a date). We'll get into dating specifics later, but the tools presented in this chapter are meant to be utilized whether you've just met someone or have been dating him for a year. But we need to find eligible bachelors before we can attract them, so, where are they?

Dear Ms. Avi,

I was out last night and met Nick, a very quirky-cute lawyer with an irresistible Jew-fro and minimal muscles. We spent all night talking about our parents in Boca and being badass back in the day at Camp Eisner. As I was leaving, he handed me a card. What do I do with this 2x3 piece of paper?

Nora

Nick Feldstein

Lawyer at Big Law Firm

777-9311

nfeldstein@biglawfirm.com

Dear Nora,

Here's what you do. Now pay attention. I'm only going to say this once. Flip the card over. Write your name and number on it. Then hand it back to him with your number written on it. Of course, if you're also a lawyer, and you would like him as a business contact, the above recipe is not recommended. If you're not a lawyer, but enjoy dating them, and would like some more "personal" contact in the future, the steps above will suit you well.

But what if Nick said, "Do you want my number?" Say, "Sure," just to be polite. Take it, but make sure to give him yours. This may sound insane to you, but erase his number from your phone. There's no need for it in your phone. You're not going to call him.

Love,
Ms. Avi

Avi

867-5309

Chapter 3-

Where to Meet a Mensch and Other Awkward Party Situations

As heartbreaking as it may be, not all Jewish guys go to *Jewish* events. Not all of them are putting on their suits and yarmulkes on Friday night and heading to Temple. To utilize your newfound shiksa appeal most effectively, you should attend both Jewish and non-specifically Jewish events. Many of our men get taken because they participate only in secular activities, so for the most part they are only meeting shiksas. Put on your sexy camouflage vest and stilettos—it's time to go hunting in some obvious and not-so-obvious places.

A Glossary Before We Go Hunting:
Here are some characters you may encounter on your mission:

Kosher Player: The smooth talking guy in town who gets with every Jewish girl because he knows he can. He touches your arm five times within the first five minutes of meeting you, and he seems a little too good to be true. He is not to be discounted, because he is oftentimes very smart and accomplished, but just be on the watch for ulterior motives.

Shark: A man in his late thirties or early forties who solely hits on women who are at least ten years his junior. Unlike the Kosher Player, the Shark has no game. If you end up in a conversation with one, you need an excuse to get out immediately (such as a made-up boyfriend). Hopefully someone who knows about the Shark will rescue you from your awkward conversation.

Self-Hating Jew: The guy who describes himself as "the worst Jew ever" and is proud of it. He will often scoff at more religious people, and probably fosters resentment towards his heritage. By definition, the Self-Hating Jew would probably not be found at a specifically Jewish event, but you will be sure to come across some of these guys in your daily interactions.

Wing-Jew: This friendly face, more commonly known as a wing-man, is your best ally in a social setting. He/she will ensure that you're not standing in the corner alone. It's probably best if your Wing-Jew is female, but use a guy friend as a last resort. Despite the fact that being surrounded by men makes you appear appealing and desirable, having a guy can sometimes backfire. It may cause a cock-block, because other men might think you are off the market. Added bonus—your Wing-Jew will assist you by removing you from conversations with undesirable men, and can introduce you to his/her friends at the event.

The events below are broken down into two basic types of events/ places:

Every Man for Himself Events (EMH): These events include happy hours, BBQ's, networking events, or house parties. For EMH events, may I suggest hiring a Wing-Jew? Another point to keep in mind is that if you're surrounded by a pack of women, a man will be more intimidated and less likely to start up a conversation. Don't be afraid to break away occasionally to get a drink. That nice lawyer may be afraid to approach you with your friends hanging around. But always be aware when you break away, a *Shark* may be lurking around the drinks table.

Forced Conversation/Activity Events (FC): These are a Ms. Avi favorite, because you are *guaranteed* to meet people and there is no work involved. Go alone (or with one friend at most), or else it hinders your ability to meet new people. There's also no need for awkward conversation-enders such as, "Oh, I have to talk to those guys now… over there…away from you." See, that was really bad. Examples of forced conversation events include hiking, board-game nights, rock climbing, Shabbat dinners, dance lessons, and Jewish learning classes. If you're new to a city (or just shy), try out one of these events to avoid being that girl standing in the corner stuffing your face with Cheetos at an EMH event—trust me, Jews remember.

Jewish Events:
Men attend Jewish events for one of the following two reasons:

1. **They are active members of the community** and are probably searching for a Jewish woman. If this weren't so, JDate would be out of business.

Or...

2. **They know their market price is higher within the Jewish singles scene.** Jewish men are well aware they have what we want (their kosherness). For all you economists out there, let's put it another way: since the demand for Jewish men is higher among Jewish females than anywhere else, these men are a more valuable commodity within our community and can garner a higher price for their "goods." Thus, a mediocre-looking and/or socially awkward Jewish guy knows he can woo a much more attractive woman at a Jewish event than he could in shiksa-land. Supply and demand, baby. ✡

Here are some ideas for settings where you can use your shiksa appeal knowing that everyone there is fair game:

1. Jewish Young Professional Events (FC, EMH)—You'll find guys here who are looking for Jewish chicks and have an appreciation for their religion/culture/heritage. Oftentimes, you'll find that the females outnumber males at these events. Don't be discouraged by bad male/female ratios—you only need one boyfriend! Keep attending events, and you'll meet more men. For a listing of Jewish young professional events in your area try...
   a. New York: Manhattan Jewish Experience
   b. DC: Gather the Jews
   c. Chicago: Jewish Federation of Metropolitan Chicago
   d. LA: Aish Los Angeles

✡ Please disregard my blatant stereotyping of only socially awkward Jewish guys being involved in Jewish events to get women. There are a few anomalous nice guys who are good-looking and involved in Jewish communities. But they probably think the sun shines out of their asses.

e. Boston: CJP Boston's Jewish Young Leadership Division

f. In a city near you: Birthright Israel NEXT

This is not an exhaustive list so check the web pages of local synagogues in your areas or Google "Young Professional Jewish Events in [insert your shtetl here]." Local Hillel directors can be good sources as well of the local Young Professional scenes, so don't be afraid to reach out.

2. Jewish Fundraisers and Events/Galas that Cost Money to Attend (FC, EMH)—Events that require payment towards a cause are sure to attract men with cash. In New York, one of the best is Young Jewish Professionals (www.yjpnewyork.org). This group runs all sorts of fundraisers and galas in the city. Outside of New York, check out the Ben Gurion Society of the Jewish Federation. This is a national donor recognition program for young professionals. If you are a member of the society, you will receive invitations to special professional and personal networking events in your area and around the country.

3. High Holiday Services (EMH)—The High Holidays are the only three days of the year when you will see most guys with any connection to Judaism wearing a kippah, except at their cousin's bar mitzvah. Look for temples with large young professional communities. Don't feel bad about looking cute for guys on Yom Kippur. Put on that form-fitting yet conservative dress and heels. Remember, God wants you to find a shul-mate, and he won't be mad if repentance isn't the only thing on your mind that day. When you're married, you can repent on Yom Kippur for having dressed a little too sexy for the Day of Atonement in the past. Also take advantage of the fact that you haven't eaten and aren't carrying around extra water weight. Going

home to be with the family for the Holidays? Don't fret, my pet. Don't be surprised if 50 percent of the young-ish looking people on your trains/planes/buses are tribesmates. Wear your Jewish star and maybe a cute guy will strike up a conversation.

4. Jewish Learning Classes (FC)—Try taking a Jewish studies class, or a Talmud or Hebrew class through your local JCC or Synagogue.

5. Formal Gatherings Involving a Rabbi and an Open Bar (FC)—Don't forget about hitting up the weddings, bar-mitzvahs, funerals, and other events where the men are forced to show up and look nice. Remember that if it's your cousin's bar mitzvah, he has another side of the family for you to date! Just double-check to make sure you're not related before getting involved.

6. Shabbat Dinners (FC)—Check your city for large organized Shabbat dinners for young professionals. Choose your tablemates wisely, because they might be the only people you talk with all night and you don't want to be stuck next to a Shark. Be sure to pick a good-looking table with guys you have not dated already! Also, be open to conversations when you get up for drinks or to get food. This is a prime opportunity to mingle with men from other tables if it is a large dinner.

7. Vacations/Cruises (EMH)—Looking to get away? There are many options to meet men away from home. Jewish guys will flock to any typical spring break location. Remember to wear your Israeli T-shirt while sipping that Margarita at the pool. Also, be sure to check out cruises and vacations specifically for Jewish singles. Check out your local JCC to see if they are running any trips in the near future (oftentimes these trips are subsidized) and don't forget about Birthright and

Birthright Alumni trips. For Jew cruises, try JSinglesCruise. com, AmazingJourneys.net, and TotallyJewishTravel.com.

If the young professionals group you're looking for doesn't exist, create it! My friend Seth went to hip-hop clubs, but always ended up taking home the types of women his mother would not approve of. He then decided to start a Jewish hip-hop dance instruction group, so he could meet Jewish girls and turn them in to hip-hop dancers. Brilliant!

Mensch-Friendly Non-Specifically Jewish Events:

What about all the guys who don't attend Jewish events? Let's tap into that market, which is oftentimes overrun with shiksas. Many Jewish guys (especially the smart, good-looking ones with good jobs) are frying their brains playing *World of Warcraft* on Friday night, football on Saturday with their buddies, and kickball during the week. So, if Moshe won't come to mountain, the mountain must come to Moshe. In other words, you must go where the non-dorky Jews go (and wear your Jewish star so that the men know you're not treif). Here is a listing of places to find Jewish guys that are not so obvious:

1. Law School (FC)—This is not a specifically *Jewish* event, but it may as well be listed as one. Shocking as it may be, there are tons of Jewish lawyers, and they all went to law school before passing the bar exam. The Catholic/Christian law schools are especially great places to meet Jewish men. The logic here is that Jewish guys have no problem going to these shiksa havens, but Jewish girls don't go because they're afraid there won't be available Jewish men. Guess again, honey.

2. Sports Leagues (FC)—Many, many Jewish men join local sports leagues. Try a soccer, frisbee, kickball, or softball league and wear a shirt with something Jewish on it. Go to

an Israeli T-shirt website, get your sister to bring you back a nice shirt from Israel, or wear a pretty Jewish star necklace. Most Jewish Community Centers also run sports leagues. Men get nachas from helping out damsels in distress. Even if you suck at basketball, join the basketball league anyway. Maybe a cute guy will help you with your free throws. Even if you don't need help, play dumb and ask anyway. Guys don't go for the butch chicks in long shorts, so no worries if your skills need improvement. In fact, being too good at sports can sometimes scare guys off.

3. Running Clubs (FC)—I don't know why, but Jewish men love running clubs. Find one in your area through the Road Runners Club of America http://www.rrca.org/find-a-running-club/.

4. Krav Maga (FC)—This hand-to-hand combat system utilized by the Israeli Defense Forces is becoming ever-more popular in the USA and is even taught in some police departments and military units. There are many Krav Maga centers located around the country, and American Jewish guys flock to these classes because it makes them think for a split second that they're badass, ripped, and tan like their Israeli brothers. Then they leave class and come back to reality.

5. Professional Societies and Mixers (EMH)—Since many of these are not specifically Jewish events, be sure to wear a pretty Magen David necklace. One of my favorites is The Ivy Plus Society where a bunch of people who went to a specific list of prestigious universities get together for drinks and snacks. They actually let anyone in, so you can still attend no matter where you went to school.

6. The Suburbs (EMH)—Go to the 'burbs or events in the 'burbs (in cities with Jewish populations) to meet marriage-

minded men who already own houses. Cha-ching! If a guy owns a house, that's a great sign he's looking for a girlfriend or wife.

7. Political Campaigns (FC)—If you prefer debating politics over playing sports, then great! Plenty of Jewish guys *love* politics. Too many, in fact. Sign up to work a campaign (Democrat or Republican), wear your Jewish star, and you will meet plenty of Jewish guys. Excuse me for throwing a Jewish event back in the mix, but another best kept secret is the Republican Jewish Coalition (http://www.rjchq.org/). As long as you're comfortable with Republicans, you'll have a field day at this politically conservative meat market.

8. Dance Class (FC)—Although this sounds counterintuitive, partner dancing classes (ballroom, salsa, or swing) can be a great place to meet men and the ratio will, in fact, not be entirely skewed. Many men without girlfriends sign up for dance classes solely because they know that they will be surrounded by single women.

9. Online and Speed-Dating (EMH)—Not all Jewish guys get their moms to pay for JDate. Find Jewish guys even on Match.com, eHarmony, and OkCupid. You'll even find them at regular (not specifically Jewish) and Asian speed-dating events. Wear your Jewish star and you'll attract them. Check out Chapter 4 for more dirt on these topics.

10. LSAT/MCAT/GMAT/GRE Prep Classes (FC)—In the 1920s, Harvard and other Ivy League schools took measures to reduce Jewish enrollment at their institutions. So what did Stanley Kaplan do? He invented SAT tutoring. An LSAT class in particular would be a great place to meet a man with future earning potential.

11. Outdoor Trips (FC)—What better place to bond than over a campfire? It goes without saying that outdoor trips

attract men. One of the best outdoor options for singles is Club Getaway in Connecticut. It'll remind you of summer camp, and they even have a few "J Weekends" specifically for tribesmates if that's more your style. Check it out at http://www.clubgetaway.com/. If you live outside of the tri-state area, your city probably has an outdoor interest group for young professionals. Remember to look sexy and wear a hint of makeup even though you feel gross sleeping in the woods. I just hope there's not a *Shark* in your tent.

12. Meetup.com/Events and Adventures: (FC, EMH)—Even non-Jewish events will have Jewish attendees. Try something dorky, intellectual, outdoorsy, sporty, or political and you will be sure to bump into a few tribesmates. Look out especially for free or cheap events—you know plenty of our kind will be there.

13. Bars (EMH)—A lot of Jewish guys do the bar thing on Friday and Saturday nights. Hell, they're even there on Monday, Tuesday, Wednesday, and Thursday nights. Don that Jewish star, and you're ready for a good time. Hit up areas that Jews would be around, but be sure to avoid the Kosher Players. Game-day is an especially great time to go.

14. The Gym (EMH)—Remember the Jewish shirt or Jewish star and you're set. Don't forget to get off that girlie elliptical for five minutes! Look around; it's chicks on the treadmills and stair-steppers. Go to the weight room. You can even enlist the help of a male friend to teach you how to lift so you can become a regular there. Oh, and don't be afraid to look semi-presentable or downright sexy in your workout attire, either.

A Word on Numbers:

You may think that you have a better shot of meeting your perfect man in New York City or in college, both places that are full of hot, good-looking, smart Jews (like the Israeli army, but with less running). But this is exactly the reason it may be harder to get asked out in those places, because they are full of hot, good-looking, smart Jewish girls. These places are stacked with competition, and unless you are Natalie Portman, you might get lost in the crowd. If you live in a big city, attend smaller events such as Shabbat dinners or join leagues or political groups to find a niche. Of course, dress sexy—and just for the record, a little concealer never killed anyone.

> Feel like you've dated every Jewish guy in DC, NY, or LA? Though you may have slightly slutty tendencies, there are Jewish men out there yet to be conquered; you just need to put yourself in different locations and situations to find them. Large cities have transient populations, so don't fret. There's always fresh meat in town.

Living in Abilene, Texas for the summer with a Jewish population of sixty? Plan weekend trips to Houston or Dallas and attend Shabbat dinners, speed-dating parties, and other Jewish events. You can find such groups by a simple Google search. Don't be ashamed to lie to everyone you meet and say, "Oh, I come to Houston at least once a month." No one will know the difference. Put up a JDate profile and list the nearest large metropolitan area as your location. Another option is to set your online location to where your family or friends live, and find more potential boyfriends in those locales. If you meet a man and there's chemistry, he won't care whether you live five or a fifty miles away.☆ Because you're from out of town, you'll be perceived as unique and a breath of fresh air. If you can tell he's interested, be upfront in your conversations and let him know you actually live in Abilene, not Houston. Let him call you a few times, and then arrange to meet up again.

My friend Sarah came from Baltimore to DC for a speed-dating event thinking that no guys would be interested because she came from far away. Despite the fact that she was geographically undesirable, she walked away with four dates from the event. Living outside the bulk of the Jewish community just makes you a challenge. A bit of self-selection never hurt anyone.

Be the New Girl in Town—Even if You've Been Here Five Years: The new girl in town is always the most attractive. When you first moved to your shtetl, you were an excited young dove asking men questions about the best restaurants and the cheapest place to get your dry-cleaning done—and now you know it all. You may have noticed how much male attention you received when you first moved to your city. Has that male attention dwindled and you find yourself being chased more frequently by *Sharks*? Too often, we get stuck in ruts where we do the same things and see the same people and fail to remove ourselves from our comfort zones.

If this describes you, then it's time to break out a pen and paper and think outside the box for new ventures to get involved with where you can be that excited young dove again. Join a political campaign, even if you can't name a single justice on the Supreme Court. You'll be the "new girl" on the campaign trail, and many guys will be eager to teach you about politics. Habitat for Humanity is a great place to ask a man for assistance and by doing so will make him feel like a regular Ty Pennington. Even if you've never used a

☆ Disclaimer: Yes, there are men who are too lazy to travel; forget about them.

hammer, you'll leave the experience with newfound skills that may or may not be useful in real life. Seek out other activities where you need a man's assistance, such as salsa dancing or rock climbing. These activities are great chemistry builders.

Work on Your Jew-dar:

Since it's not 1891, and the majority of our men have lost their eastern European fashion trends (long coats, black hats), it is more difficult to spot tribesmates. Spotting a Jew is an art—an art called *Jew-dar*. This skill can't be taught overnight, but practice makes perfect (unless he's an African-American convert). Jew-dar is part looks, part name, and part neuroticism. If he's antsy about whether the cookies have nuts and will give him rashes, you may have a Jew on your hands.

How do you make sure? Say you're at your soccer league game, and after talking for a while with Mike, the hottest guy on the team, you throw in something about your last trip to Israel. Mention that you're building a Sukkah with your friends or missing the game next week for Passover. See if he bites. If he does, you have your answer.

Lucky for us, there are ten names that Jewish guys have, so half the battle is over once you find out his first name: David, Daniel, Ari, Eli, Josh, Jared, Michael, Marc (c or k), Zach (h), Jon (no h), and Ben. Unfortunately, the goyim have adopted these popular Torah names as well. Michael Jordan is, in fact, not Jewish. When you meet someone named Jesse, Patrick, Billy-Beau, Chris, Pablo, or Mohammed, there's a low chance he had a bar mitzvah (although Ms. Avi has met attractive Jewish males with the name Chris, so don't throw in the towel immediately).

We all know about Jewish last names. But again, don't write off anyone just because his last name is Robinson. As we all know, many last names were changed at Ellis Island—or someone's father may be a goy. Also, people with Middle Eastern last names are tricky.

Rule of thumb: if the name makes you crave a falafel, then he's most likely not Jew. Fortunately, there is that ray of hope that he might be Sephardic.

Just like names, looks and behaviors can give you hints as well. Is he a Brillo head?—probably Jewish. Wearing a suit when everyone else is in jeans?—probably Jewish. The most obnoxious loud-mouth on your soccer team?—most likely a Jew. The other guy on the team without social skills?—probably Jewish as well. It's a tough world, but keep practicing. You'll never 100% be able to spot every Jew, but hopefully your Jew-Dar will improve over time.

The important take-home message from this chapter is that men don't live under rocks, and neither should you. Instead of only going to synagogue, find an activity you love to do (or want to learn to do), and use that as an excuse to have some fun and maybe meet a few keepers wearing kippot along the way. If you live in an area devoid of Chosen People, then you will have to think outside the box and make the effort to put yourself out there through other means such as online and speed-dating. Finally, listen to Ms. Avi: remember to look hot!

Dear Ms. Avi,

Is it wrong for me to go to Jewish events to meet men and make new friends even if I'm a "bagel Jew"—not too knowledgeable about the religious aspects?

Eva

Dear Eva,

Very few young professionals go to Jewish events to be Jewish. If they were going to Jewish events to be religious, you'd find young professionals at suburban synagogues on Friday nights. Try going to a suburban synagogue on a Friday night; it's all families and super-old people. Going to Jewish events alone never perpetuated the Jewish race. Going to Jewish events in a hot red dress with the men around you being force-fed copious amounts of alcohol *has* helped perpetuate the Jewish people. There's no shame in this, none at all. You may even learn about your heritage while you're there as well. When you're married, you can go to Jewish events for religious reasons.

Love always, Avi

Chapter 4-

Online, Speed-Dating, and Set-Ups: Toto, We're Not in the Old Country Anymore

If you find that you don't meet Jewish men naturally, don't despair; you're alive at a fortuitous time. We have speed-dating and the Internet, which allow you to meet men outside of your shtetl. Although professional yentas are not as prevalent as during the time of *Fiddler on the Roof,* set-ups are always an option, as well. We women aren't getting any younger. Seriously, we're not. You don't want to end up forty and alone, so take advantage of these tools while you're young and sexy. You'll have a real advantage in the playing field and some shiksa won't get to your dream man before you do. This chapter will teach you the tricks and tips of online dating, speed-dating, and set-ups.

Date Like a Shiksa in Cyberspace:

Succumbing to the pressure from your mother to join JDate doesn't mean you're a loser. It simply means that you enjoy free meals and dating multiple guys at once. Just because you have a profile up on the Internet doesn't mean you have to become a hermit. Sure, you may get one (or five) guys coming up to you at your next Shabbat dinner saying, "Hey, did I see you on JDate?" But you will not regret attending in-person events as well, and you should continue to meet guys in the real world. Online dating is also super-fabulous because you'll meet men online whom you may never have come across in your daily life. The love of your life may be someone in a nearby city, whose path you may not have crossed without the help of the Internet. Sure, you won't have as cool of a "how did you meet" story, but at least you'll have love and won't die alone an old maid.

Our Men Join Online Dating Sites Because They Are:
- ✡ Weird—can't get girls to talk to them.
- ✡ New in town.
- ✡ Busy, busy, busy.
- ✡ Living in an area with a small Jewish community

On Which Sites Can You Buy Kosher Beef?

There are two types of dating sites where you will find eligible tribesmates.

1. Pay Sites: There are many pay sites where you can meet Jewish men. In general, the more expensive a site, the more marriage-minded it is (such as eHarmony). If your JDate profile is collecting dust and not getting too many hits, then it might be time to try a different Jewish site or

Secrets of Shiksa Appeal

A World Outside of JDate?:

Yes, there are Jewish dating sites besides JDate. Here are some of them that have the most positive reviews:

✡ JewishCafe—A warm, inviting environment. This site is becoming more and more popular.

✡ Jewster—A new social network for young active Jews.

✡ Frumster—Orthodox and marriage-minded.

✡ Jewish Friend Finder—Part of the larger Friend Finder network. With 82,000+ Jewish members, you might find one to your liking.

✡ JRetroMatch—Online Jewish dating through a matchmaker.

---

even a non-specifically Jewish site. By putting your sexy picture on a non-specifically Jewish site, you'll be tapping into a group of men the other Jewish girls (who only go on Jewish sites) are neglecting. Even though eHarmony is typically thought of as a Christian site, there is the option of only being matched with Jews. If you're looking for a bagel Jew, then Match.com may be for you. I know a few kosher beefcakes who've done Match.com (one Supreme Court clerk, in fact). But you will get a fair share of Pablos sending you winks.

2. Free Sites: Since you are Jewish, it's a fair assumption that you are cheap—oh, I mean economically cautious (so I don't have the ADL coming after me). It may be tempting to post your profile on a free online dating site such as PlentyOfFish, or OkCupid. What I'm about to say may sound sacrilegious, but please use a site that requires payment, or at a minimum, payment from men.

The Perfect Pictures that Get You Free Meals:
Men only look at profiles of women they find attractive, so make sure your picture looks good! Have one headshot in addition to one photo that shows your body and that says, "Hey, I have a rockin' body." More than four pictures might look like you're *really* into this online dating thing. Also, be aware that men are wary of women with just a headshot—and for good reason. Women with one headshot and no body shot are fat. These women may actually have great bodies, but in a man's mind, if there's no body shot, it's because they're fat.

Ms. Avi's Honorary Fifth Passover Question:
"How are men who pay for dating sites different from men who don't pay?"

If he's not paying, he's either A) Cheap; B) Not serious; or C) Just trying to get laid.
Do you want a guy like that?
If he is paying, he is A) Serious about meeting someone; or B) Just trying to get laid by girls with money.
See, with option 2, there's the chance that he's not cheap and not just trying to get with you. No promises, but at least there's hope!

Believe it or not, your smile is the most important feature of your picture, even more important that your boobs. Your smile will catch his eye. There's a difference between a fake smile and a real one. If you need to, get a professional picture taken. You may pay for it now, but if you find a rich husband, I'm sure it will be worth the investment. Enlisting the help of a friend to take picture is another viable option as well. Be made up, but don't make it obvious. If you have a hobby, the second picture can be of you doing your hobby (as long as your hobby is not your ex). Soccer, tennis, chess, and painting are good examples. Men love women with a passion for their jobs and hobbies, and a picture is a great way to display yours.

If you are on the heavier side (and let's be honest, sometimes us Jewish chicks eat a few too many matzo balls), having the body shot there will make sure you're being honest, and will attract men who like curvaceous women. Men are not beyond standing you up if they see you and discover you're not exactly what was promised in the advertisement. If you are large, by being honest (a word I rarely use in dating) you're more likely to find the "chubby chaser" of your dreams.

Let's Write a Bunch of Lies, Shall We?:

As for the unimportant writing, the task of describing yourself can seem rather daunting. Here's where you bring out the easygoing shiksa inside of you, whose profile doesn't scream *marry me*. A stereotypical Jewish profile includes the word "family" at least five times. The word "family," in the mind of a Jewish male, means "babies." Of course you want a man who eventually wants babies, but no Jewish man will want you if you mention babies in your profile. Think about it another way. You want sex, but wouldn't you get creeper vibes from a man who mentions boobs in a profile? Same difference. So if you can't talk about your future children's names, what does a shiksa talk about in cyberspace?

Shiksas talk about passions and having a good time. Men love women who love what they do, even if it's working at the GAP. If you love selling clothes, then you are content with your life and will not leach onto his life. Mentioning sports you play or teams you follow never hurt anyone either. When creating a profile, try to be the girl he can watch the Packers game with but who will also dress up pretty, even if you're not this type of girl at all. Stay positive and give off the image of being content with your full life. And leave out talk of soul mates or Dr. Phil.

As for how to write about yourself, let me introduce you to two words in the English language that will enhance your profile immensely: "mystery" and "anecdote." As opposed to stating a laundry list of adjectives that may or may not actually describe you (such as, "Hi I'm a fun-loving, smart, passionate, funny, beautiful, confident chick"), give him a short anecdote about something you've done that shows your true colors. "I once spent three days/nights alone in the woods of New Zealand." This sentence would attract outdoorsy guys in a more powerful way than saying, "I'm outdoorsy." This now sets him up to ask about my trip to New Zealand.

The *mystery* part of your profile will intrigue him and gives him something to e-mail you about. I once mentioned a "unique part-time job" in a profile, but didn't give any other details about the job. I probably had ten men write to me asking what my unique job entailed. (I'm sure they were hoping it was stripping). Mention in your profile that you "grew up in a small town that only five people in DC have heard of." It changes you from "just another typical Jewish girl" into a "challenge," and will leave him asking the name of your town. Anyone is capable of adding anecdotes and mystery to shiksify their profile.

Reading, Responding, and the Shiksa Shabbat:

Now that your profile makes you appear to be the Jewish version of Mila Kunis (oh snap, she is Jewish), you're ready to answer the men who send you messages.

So you've received a personalized message written to you (not a form letter) that mentions one or two pieces of information from your profile and not your enormous bustline. Mazal tov, he actually read your profile and responded. Good start. There's really only one rule for responding to an e-mail, and that is to keep it short and sweet, writing less than he wrote. You don't have to answer all of his questions. He's not looking to read a book; he just likes your picture.

Besides what you write in your messages, a man will take into consideration the time it takes you to respond. You may be sitting by your computer all day, but he doesn't have to know that. Even I'd be suspicious of a guy who e-mailed me back ten seconds after I sent him a message. Please wait a few hours before replying to his messages so he thinks you're a busy girl with an active life. Just as we Jews have our Shabbat, the shiksas have their own Shabbat, which we call the *Shiksa Shabbat*. It lasts from Friday night through Sunday at 4:00 p.m. During the Shiksa Shabbat, the shiksa does not log onto online dating websites to check or send messages. She pretends to be busy with dates, Church, more dates, and eating ham sandwiches. Not too much time left for her to be checking online dating sites Saturday afternoon.

Another important skill when conversing with men online is an ability to weed out the time-wasters.✿ Some men feel cool talking to women online, may have no interest in actually meeting them, and probably have no social skills and don't look like their pictures; these men are time-wasters.

First Encounters of the Jewish Male Kind:

Meeting a guy that you've shared e-mail exchanges with for the first time can make anyone uneasy. But it's better to do it sooner rather than later, because chemistry can only be built in person (and a little over the phone). Some profiles are very misleading. The one picture posted of him looks normal, and his five-word e-mail seems nice enough: "You sound cool, let's meet for dinner."

✿   The term, *time-waster,* was originally coined in 2002 by Sherrie Schneider and Ellen Fein in *The Rules for Online Dating,* and has been saving women online from pathetic men ever since.

Ms. Avi's Clues That He's Wasting Your Time:

✡ Doesn't mention anything about you or your profile specifically in his email.

✡ Sends a "flirt," but no message.

✡ Is online all the time.

✡ Waits too long to respond (more than three days)—without an excuse like he's in Israel fighting Hamas.

✡ Says, "Read my profile to find out," when you ask him about his hobbies.

✡ Doesn't ask you out after his fourth or fifth message—he's probably looking for a pen pal or email buddy, not a date.

✡ Posts pictures that are *too* good and there are way too many of them.

✡ Is online while you're at work. Men online in the middle of the day are bums looking for their sugar mama. Doesn't he have something more important to be doing?

✡ Lives in Cali, and you live in NY.

✡ Doesn't ask for your e-mail address or ask if he can contact you again at the end of the IM conversation.

To avoid wasting your time and gas on a loser, please follow these two rules when meeting an online guy in person for the first time:

✡ Secret #1 is to get him on the phone before you meet him in person. If you've already agreed to meet, you can even say, "Call me and we can figure out when/where we're meeting." That way, if he turns out to be Mr. Bean on the phone, you can cancel. If he asks you out via e-mail, you can say, "Sure, I'm free Wednesday. Give me a call sometime, so

we can work out a time/place. My number is 867-5309."
Coordinating is easier over the phone, and you have the
added bonus of making sure he has social skills.

✡ Secret #2 is to go for coffee, drinks, or a walk for the first
date. Then there's always the excuse, "Oops, I gotta run;
have to walk the dog," if it's not going well. If you end up
doing a meal instead, it means you have to spend two hours
with him. Coffee could last just as long, but at least there's
a way out.

Slap Yourself Sometimes:
Avoid getting giddy like a schoolgirl about a guy you've never
met:

✡ There's a 90 percent chance he's not all that.

✡ He might weigh 100 pounds more than advertised.

✡ You may freak him out by acting like your relationship
is bigger than it is, when you've never met.

Before the date, calm yourself down. Online dating used to be
only for losers and freaks, but now everyone does it. If it goes really
badly (and there's a high probability that it might), then at least you
have a good story. Just play it cool, and let him pay. If he asks you
to split the bill, open your wallet this once, and then never go out
with him again. Find a meeting location that's convenient for you,
so if it's a complete waste of an hour, at least you didn't add on an
hour of driving time.

After a few months, if things are slow on JDate, remove your
profile and try another site. It'll be just like you're the new girl
in town again!

Facebook, LinkedIn, and Other Stalking Mechanisms:
Social networking sites are a double-edged sword in today's dating world. There's not much stopping your pretty little finger from clicking and finding out his sister's name, where he interned after college, and how many girlfriends he's had in the past year. Sure, you can look at his picture all day long, but you might also find out information about him that he has not yet told you, and inadvertently mention it during the date. Now you look like a stalker. Even though you've probably marked up his JDate profile with a highlighter, put on your shiksa hat and pretend as if you've never read his profile (whether it's Facebook, JDate, or LinkedIn) in much detail. Using online mechanisms (such as Facebook) to find out his life story is a possible chemistry killer. Proceed with caution!

But wait, there's more! If there's a guy you're interested in, online, offline, or even your LSAT tutor, ensure that your Facebook privacy settings are set so that he can only view your main profile picture and basic information. Don't allow him the pleasure of staring at photos of you in a bikini all day long. Also by blocking your profile and photos, you ensure he cannot see pictures of you and your ex-boyfriends.

Wait as long as possible to confirm Facebook friendship. Don't accept a man's friend request until you've met in person. If he requests friendship before you've even met him, it's fine to ignore the request until he gets to know you better. It won't stop him from calling you. He may think you're aloof and not obsessed with him, which is a good, shiksa quality. Part of the fun of dating is making him work to find out about you. If he knows all your favorite movies and books from Facebook, what else is there for him to ask?

As for pictures, remove any that make you look like a slut (but isn't that obvious?). No guy wants to see you kissing other guys or that wet T-shirt contest you competed in. The key is to not give out too much information, either via Facebook or an online dating profile.

You goal is to keep the mystery and intrigue alive. Let him find out that you speak fluent Mandarin from you, not the Internet.

Speed-Dating 101:

Just saying these words brings up images of short, balding men with serious hygiene issues. But that's really not the case, so get those thoughts out of your head! So you'll meet a few weirdos while speed-dating, but you would at *any* Jewish event. If you attended a Jewish event and met "normal" guys, you'd be thinking, *This isn't a Jewish event; it's a bunch of imposters!*

Here's the scoop on speed-dating: you'll have anywhere from ten to twenty mini-dates in the session (lasting anywhere from four to seven minutes each). If you like each other, you write each other's name/ID number down. After the event there will be a way to communicate with event participants who you were least disgusted by. Within the time span of 1 hour, you may walk away with a few dates lined up for next week—now that's efficiency!

Not sure what to chat about? Attraction is pretty blatant. If you're looking for an artsy guy, ask which museums in the city he enjoys. If you're looking for sporty, then ask about his favorite football team. If it's not a match, he'll say he doesn't really like sports, and you know you can continue the "uh huhs" and "yeahs" and really be thinking about what to say to the next guy. People always say that you shouldn't ask a man, "What do you do?" during speed-dating. Rumor has it that this innocent phrase is sometimes interpreted as, "How big a ring do you plan on buying me?" I don't buy this at all. At some point, you should find out what the fresh meat sitting a foot away from you does during the day. The truth is that only men with jobs/careers go to speed-dating events because they know they will be asked this question. No man wants to repeat he's "between jobs" fifteen times in one hour.

You may be asking, "Ms. Avi, there are many different sorts of events. Which speed-dating should I attend?" Don't limit yourself to Jewish-only events. Go to any type based on what's comfortable for you. There are age-based events as well as interest-based events (travel, food, fitness). But of course, don't leave home without wearing the pretty Jewish star for an extra edge over the competition at the interest or age-based events. If he's a tribesmate, he'll be sure to compliment you on it and he'll be refreshed to meet such a beautiful, well-spoken, and calm Jewish chick.

Some Jewish guys are scared of Jewish speed-dating events, and by attending a non-specifically Jewish event, you will be tapping into a market that other women are neglecting. I know many nice Jewish guys who feel more comfortable at non-religious speed-dating events because Judaism is not a major part of their lives at the current time. However, once a Jew, always a Jew. I once met a couple at services who met at a non-specifically Jewish speed-dating event. His father is Jewish, and he never explored his religion. They are now engaged and he is studying for his bar-mitzvah.

Think outside the box and consider going to events where you'll have a competitive edge age-wise over the competition. If you're twenty-eight, think about events for people in their thirties. If the range is twenty-five to thirty-five and you go when you're twenty-five, even though you may feel too young, you have more dating opportunities than any other woman in the room. In a man's eyes, young = fertile. And fertile = hot. The women in the room may give you dirty looks, but pay no attention to them; you're there for the men.

What to Wear to Speed-Dating:

I know we touched on this in Chapter 1, but what you wear is half the battle. First impressions count, especially in a one-time-meeting situation such as speed-dating. Men are attracted to colors and feminine, form-fitting clothes. Men will remember you as the beautiful woman in the blue dress. Work that shiksa look and dress for the men. But here's the clincher: dress as if you're going on a first date at the venue.

Once, a woman showed up in a black cocktail dress to a speed-dating event at a coffee shop; she was completely out of place. A casual dress or skirt works well at a coffee shop. If the event is held on a Saturday night at a bar, then sexified dresses are appropriate.

Hire a Wing-Jew for the Night:

If you're awkward (which is highly likely, given that you're Jewish), bring a fellow single friend along to the event. There will most likely be up to thirty minutes of mixing and mingling before the speed-dating begins, and you'll have a Wing-Jew to hang around the bar with. (It's also a lot of fun to gossip afterward about the men you met.) But sit separately once the dating begins, so as to not distract each other by making funny faces. If you're comfortable going alone, then that is a good option, as well.

After the Awkwardness Ends:

No matter which type of speed-dating event it is (mutual match or other), let the men contact you. You may receive a few e-mails like this:

Hey Avi,
I enjoyed meeting you, and would like to get to know you beyond the four minutes (haha!).
I can be reached at IreallyDontCare87@gmail.com.
Greg

Ms. Avi's beef with this message is: 1) It's cliché, and 2) It doesn't show that he remembered anything about me! He remembers being at the event and meeting lots of women, but not me. Unless you had some great connection with him, or know him through friends, this is the kind of e-mail you reply back to with, "Sorry, I'm really busy this week. I don't think I'll be able to meet up." The following is the type of message you want to reply to:

Hey Avi,

I enjoyed meeting you on Wednesday, and think it's cool that you play soccer, too. Let's meet up next Friday for dinner.

Greg

This message shows that he was paying attention to something besides your boobs during the four minutes. Only reply to men who seem to have remembered something about you, otherwise, they really didn't care. And remember to leave the week following speed-dating open for potential dates. First dates need not be on a Saturday. Sometimes you'll meet lots of great men during one night of speed-dating. Other times, the pickings may be slim, and there may be no future fathers for your unborn children at the event. But don't give up hope. Keep putting yourself out there.

Set-ups—The Other White Mitzvah:

Now this book is to help you find love, but this is also about us Jewish chicks (even the Jappy ones) sticking together and helping each other out when it comes to set-ups. Here's why: if you set up a friend with a cute guy you used to date, she is more likely to set you up with a cute guy she used to date. It's called sharing, and sharing is caring. It's a mitzvah, just like giving Tzedakah. Your friends are not jumping out of their seats to set you up? Ask! Either they don't want to set you up, don't know anyone, or didn't know that you'd be up for it. Don't be afraid to ask your Jewish male friends or Gentile friends, either. Men are less likely to say out of the blue, "Yeah, I have this cute smart friend, Jason. He's a real catch." See? Kind of fruity. But even guys you're not too close with may make an effort to help if you ask.

How to Be Set Up:

So your Asian friend from work, Lue-Ming, says she knows a guy who would be perfect for you. Or, at least, you're Jewish, he's Jewish, and you're the only two Jews she knows. So therefore you must be perfect for each other. Ask Lue-Ming to show you a picture of the potential Yid, and have her show him a picture of you. That way, if you know you're not interested, you're not wasting anyone's time. Meet for coffee or a drink (much like a first online date) so if there's no chemistry, you're not trapped for a two-hour dinner thinking, *I hate Lue-Ming, I hate Lue-Ming, kill me now.* Just go in hoping to make a new friend and nothing more. Don't get your hopes up. You'll probably have a miserable time.

People often forget after a particularly horrible blind date to send Lue-Ming (or whichever Asian set you up) a thank-you e-mail for attempting a mitzvah. Remember, your friend went out on a limb to set you up. If, by some strange monstrosity, the date did work out, thank the friend, as well. Be sure not to give too many details or sound too giddy about the guy, or else your friend will blab to the guy and say you called to say you've picked out the wedding dress. Keep in mind that every time someone sets up friends, he/she takes a risk with minimal potential reward (besides eating too many pastry puffs at their wedding someday). So thank your friend for taking a risk.

Step-by-Step Instructions on How to Perform a Set-Up:

✡ Step 1: E-mail the guy asking if he'd be interested in a set-up, and be sure to attach an attractive picture of the female. He's more likely to say no (because men can sometimes be anti-set-ups), so ask him first. Wait for him to say either "hot" or "busted." Most guys are not very discriminatory based on a picture, and will give it two Torahs up.

✡ Step 2: E-mail the girl with a picture of the guy and a little information about his job. This is the time to randomly throw in names of Ivy League institutions or any other applicable information. Wait for her approval, though you probably don't need it because most women are beyond ecstatic to be set up.

✡ Step 3: Send her e-mail or phone number to the guy. Do not send his contact info to her! Make him call or e-mail her. Tell them to meet up for coffee or drinks near her. You don't want to be held responsible for it being, "the *worst* two-hour dinner of my life. He spent the whole time staring at my chest and talking about Joe Lieberman."

✡ Step 4: Pat yourself on the back; you've just performed a mitzvah.

I hope this chapter encouraged you to take advantage of the abundant opportunities to meet men and not be afraid to use modern technology to your advantage. Get out of the habit of thinking that only losers and socially awkward people use the Internet, speed-dating, and set-ups. Stop thinking that you can only meet your soul mate by almost getting run over in the street, like how Charlotte met Trey on *Sex and the City*. Remember, they got divorced. *Then* she met Harry.

Dear Ms. Avi,

I've been dating Marc for a month or so now. I just checked Match. com, and his profile is still up. Do I confront him?

Love, Jackie

Dear Jackie,

You log on to see if he's logged on, and he logs on to see if you're logged on. It's a vicious and ridiculous cycle. The obvious answer here is that if you're dating exclusively, then your eHarmony, JDate, Match, and OkCupid profiles must all come down as soon as the "exclusivity talk" is had (see Chapter 5).

But what if you have not yet had the "exclusivity talk?" Asking a man if his profile is still up is essentially asking him "are we exclusive?" As we will discuss later, a month is too early to bring up this topic of discussion.

If you really like Marc, then just log in once every few days if you have new messages to answer from other men. Otherwise, just don't bother logging in and hopefully the "exclusivity talk" will come soon enough. Whatever you do, don't go editing your profile and changing your pictures at this point. If he sees your new profile he'll take it as a clear sign that you're seriously looking elsewhere and not interested in him.

Love Always, Avi

Chapter 5-

Date Like a Shiksa

Here we'll delve into ways to shiksify your act and to act like the un-desperate Jewish femme fatale you are (or at least pretend to be). There are no second chances to blow him away and make a great first impression. You have to create memories of positive dates where he is able to show off and provide. The dating rituals also provide you with an opportunity to really get to know him and decide if he is worth your time without rushing into the physical. The shiksa plays off the first few dates in a light, refreshing, upbeat, sexy manner, and so shall you.

How to Handle the "Where Should We Meet?" Dilemma:
If he suggests a place for the date that would require you to drive an hour to get to, here's the time to bring out your inner shiksa. A shiksa would not drive an hour out of her way for a first or second date. You can respond coyly by saying, "Are there any restaurants closer to [insert your shtetl here] that we could try?" If he drives, suggest that

he pick you up. If he doesn't drive, then really push to meet someplace convenient for you that's near public transportation. Leslie was asked out by a guy who lived in Maryland while she lived in Virginia. He suggested that they meet at a Smithsonian museum in DC for a date. Leslie brought out her inner shiksa and said, "Sorry, I'm really swamped this week; can we do Virginia?" He agreed.

Sometimes men will say, "You know your area better than I do; I'll let you pick." The key here is to pick someplace low-key and not too pricey. Only an inconsiderate JAP would pick out the most expensive restaurant in the neighborhood. If you're meeting for drinks, a brewery is a good choice because men love beer. Another option is to give him three choices of local places such as a pizzeria, a Mexican restaurant, and a brewery. That way, he thinks he planned the date and feels masculine and in control—while, in actuality, you were in control and get to eat a one of your favorite local restaurants.

What about the case where planes, trains, or teleporters are involved in facilitating your budding romance? The same rules apply to long-distance dating. Make sure the location for the first two dates is convenient for you. If you met on your family trip to Miami and you live in NY, then by no means should you be flying back to Miami to visit him before he has flown to NY. If he says, "Come visit me; I'll take you to the Everglades," simply reply back, "How about NY for the weekend?" If he resists, then he's just not interested enough.

In addition to not traveling long distances to meet him, also avoid playing chauffeur. Remember, men pick up and drive women. Men view driving as manly, so don't emasculate or scare him with your neurotic Jewish woman driving skills. (You can't fake shiksa on this one.) The one exception would be my legally blind grandfather, who required women to drive him around his whole life.

After a few dates, you can trade off visiting each other in your respective shtetls. It's also a bit of self-selection if he lives far away from you. If he likes you, he'll make the effort despite the distance. And under no circumstances should you say before a first date, "Well, I happen to be coming to [insert his shtetl here] on Saturday night anyway." Make yourself challenging, and he will stay interested! If he's not crazy about you, he'll find a chick that lives closer.

Ms. Avi's Rule of "Who the Hell Cares?"
Do you know that girl who says, "I wish Jason would stop asking me out via text." This is silly. It's not about *how* he contacts you; it's about *whether* or not he asks you out—be it via phone, text, or sky writing. Some women obsess over the details, such as, "What a douche; he always e-mails me." He obviously cared enough to want to pay for your $15 movie and popcorn, so be happy.

Wait, When, Where: You're Picking Me Up Saturday at 6:00, Right?
So it's 5:00 p.m. on Saturday night and he said he'd meet you at TGI Fridays at 8:00 p.m, but you haven't heard from him since Tuesday. What do you do? Show up at TGI Fridays and assume that he'll be there, too? It's a tough call. Most responsible men will re-confirm a date via e-mail or text at some point before the date.

There's no need to remind guys when you're supposed to get together for a date. If he forgot or didn't bother to contact you, it just means he didn't care that much. One guy I met on JDate suggested that we get together for dinner the following Thursday at TGI Fridays. Well, Thursday rolled around, and there was no word from him, so I texted him asking if we were still on for that night. He said, "Well, I hadn't heard from you, so I assumed you weren't interested, but I'm free if you still want to meet up." Foolishly, I said, "Sure." We had a nice dinner. Big surprise, he never called again...If he had really cared about me in the slightest, he would have re-confirmed the date a few days before or the day of. My bad. I wasted my time, but at least I got a free meal at TGI Fridays.

Acting Like a Shiksa:

They say that when you really like someone, there are no rules. Ms. Avi says, "Hell, no." Men are actually scared off pretty easily by certain behaviors, and may not get the chance to know you or chase you if you display some of these dating faux pas.

Refer back to Chapter 2, and think calm, cool, and collected while you're on a date. Hold back the urge to giggle like a Hebrew school girl because you just want to devour that nice guy sitting next to you. Act like that shiksa who really couldn't care less that he's Jewish. Even if he's out of your league, if he asked you out, you're in the same league, so show no fear and keep him believing that you're to be won! Trust the Avi; if you believe it, so will he.

Acting calm, cool, and collected means acting as if going on a date is a normal occurrence, even if it's been a year since your last close encounter with the Jewish male kind. Elliot once went on a date with a girl who obviously did not get taken out a lot because she said, "You're the only man besides my grandpa who's ever bought me flowers!" Please don't. If you play it cool, he'll believe that you were prom queen—the one girl every guy wants to date (besides all of the Lakers girls).

Leave the JAP at Home:

In addition to being feminine, being appreciative goes a long way. Break the stereotype. When he opens the door, say, "Thank you." Laugh, even if he's not funny. It'll make him feel like he's showing you a good time and that he's manly. When he pays the bill, say, "Thank you for dinner." That is enough to win his heart if he's into you. Guys who like you will want to take care of you and buy you dinner, and won't expect anything in return besides an acknowledgement and to hear that you had a good time.

Let your easygoing shiksa side shine by never complaining about anything on the first few dates. Even if the food sucked, the waiter spilled red wine on you, and you waited forty-five minutes for the check, still don't complain. Find the good in every situation, such as, "The waiter is cute" (okay, don't say that), "The cappuccino was delicious," or, "Great choice for a restaurant."

Play the Dumb Blonde Card...Smartly:

At some point during your date, you two might actually have to speak to each other (unless, of course, it's a movie date). Remember that it's not an interview, so don't fire too many questions at a man at once. Asking a man too many questions about himself is a direct indicator of interest. Examples include, "What's your favorite food?," "Who's your favorite band?," or, "How old is your sister?" Of course, if he asks you one of these questions, you can ask him the same question back, but there is a more creative and manipulative way to get him talking without annoying him. That is by letting him talk about his areas of expertise and pretending to be really interested.

All men want to give advice and feel needed and competent. Instead of asking, "Where do you run?" ask a technical question that lets him show off his knowledge. If he's a computer scientist, ask him about Linux. If he's a lawyer, ask about the upcoming election. If he's a doctor, ask if those bumps are herpes—okay, no. If you don't have the same area of expertise, do research before the date, so you have an intelligent question about his field to ask or can share an interesting piece of knowledge. Sam (a lawyer) was impressed when I (a consultant) knew that Louis D. Brandeis was the first Jewish Supreme Court justice. The point is not to show off, but to show that you find his field of work interesting and challenging—so interesting that it makes him feel smart to be in it.

Another date tip…have a few conversation topics in the back of your mind pre-prepared from either your daily life or whatever's going on in the news. Your date may have a brain fart, so it never hurts to have something in the back of your mind to fill silences. You spent all that time picking out an outfit, spend a few minutes considering possible conversation topics.

The Shiksa Compliment:

Complimenting a guy on a date gives you brownie (kugel) points. I'm not talking about, "You have beautiful eyes" or, "You have a nice smile." Those are personal "direct" compliments specifically about him, which will only inflate his already-huge Jewish ego. Instead, win him over with a shiksa compliment. In other words, compliment *things*, but not him directly. Men really do fall for this bologna. Compliment the food, compliment the movie you just saw, or compliment the wine. Anything *he* has provided is fair game to compliment. The reason we give compliments on things instead of him is because it helps him feel like a solid provider and prevents you from showing too much interest. See below for some examples of shiksa compliments that will really get him excited:

Examples of Shiksa Compliments:

- ✡ After the movie he took you to: "That movie was really well written."
- ✡ During dinner at a restaurant: "The wine is nice; what year is it?"
- ✡ When he cooks for you: "The steak is so tender."
- ✡ At the harbor: "This view of the city is amazing."
- ✡ At his apartment: "I really like this couch; something about plaid really does it for me."
- ✡ And "nice car!" could never hurt.

Let the Insecure Jewish Boy Shine:

His goal on the date is to show that he could potentially provide for you and give you a comfortable life, even if he lives in his parents' basement. According to one prominent New York bachelor, "It's no secret that Jewish women are well-educated and driven, but a successful woman is not always a plus in a man's eyes. She may, in fact, intimidate him." Make it clear that you're not trying to impress him with your material goods or high paycheck. Even if he's not, let him think he's smarter than you. Remember, he's trying to impress you! Don't tell him you make $100,000 a year and drive a Benz. He should be talking about *his* Benz.

How do you, that sexy shiksa lookalike, do this, you might ask? Men want to provide, so let them. Go back to his place, not yours. Try to be less showy than he is. For example, even if you can afford the BMW, buy the Honda. Don't talk about your family's yacht trip in the Mediterranean. Alternatively, you could talk about the road trip you took last summer. The one area you should try to impress with is with your looks. Instead of spending your savings on a coupe, spend it on clothes and Botox if you need it—something that makes you look better so guys will notice you. If he provides and you look good, you'll live happily ever after.

Another Ms. Avi Tip: Make him feel manly by going on dates that make him look like a stud muffin! If you don't ski but he does, then let him take you skiing so he can show off his *skilz*.

Positive and Happy, Even if You're Not:

You might think it's cute and funny to be witty and sarcastic. In your date's world, it's cute and funny to be positive, even when things suck. And if something in your life sucks, don't tell him. No *Bitter Betties* allowed on the date! If your dog just died yesterday, pretend it didn't happen, unless he asks. If he says, "Do you have any pets?" you can say, "I had a dog, Schmuel; he was a great dog and I loved him very much. He was sick, so it was the right time for him to go." Put a positive spin on everything! But avoid talking about the dead Schmuel if you can. If your job sucks, say, "It might not be right long-term, but I like the people I work with and I am learning a lot." Even if he's bitter and sarcastic, he wants a positive girl!

And When the Check Comes ...

If it's a date in his eyes, he will pick it up. Remember the male desire to provide? If you had an awful time and feel bad about making him pay, you can offer to pay for your share of the meal. But if you want another date, don't pull that feminist BS and keep your hands out of your purse.

> All those women's rights activists were not thinking of their bank accounts when they insisted that men treat them as equals and started pretending to awkwardly pull out their wallets at the end of dates.

If the date includes dinner, dancing, and a trip to Ben & Jerry's, you can offer to pay for a small portion, such as a cup of *Phish Food* ice cream. It's a pleasure for him to feel manly and pay. If he's a nerdy Jewish guy, how else can he feel manly besides opening his wallet? He's not going to save anyone from a burning building anytime soon. But make sure to say thank you once he puts down that credit card (which will hopefully be used to buy you many more nice things in the future). Once you have been out at least four times, it is then alright to reciprocate with a home-cooked dinner or tickets to an inexpensive concert or sporting event. But please do not spend too much money on him!

Once Kate went out to dinner after a volleyball game with a friend with whom she hoped to become more than friends. They split a chicken and had great conversation. Kate was sure she was on a date; unfortunately he wasn't on a date. When the bill came, he picked it up, put a $10 bill in, and then handed it to her so she could pay her share. Kate later found out he had no feelings for her. Ms. Avi's rule of thumb: if he ever plans to get with you, he's picking up the bill for dinner. Not because he has to, but because men get great joy from taking care of the women they hope to get with someday.

Leave Him Wanting More:
Men want to want you. At the end of every date, he should be thinking, "Man, I had a great time with this girl. I want to see her again." When you overstay your welcome, you're more likely to end on a sour note, or an, "I've seen enough of her today" note. If you want to stay at his apartment for four hours, leave after three. Ending all encounters first is the safe way to go. Guys hate awkwardness—the awkwardness of ending a phone call, the awkwardness of ending a date by saying, "No, thanks, I don't want to go upstairs." By ending everything first, you always leave him wanting more.

"Are You Going to Call Me? *Please?*"
My friend said this to a date once; please refrain from doing so. If he asks you out on the spot to get together again, that's great. If not, don't fret. Many guys fear in-person rejection, and will wait to call/e-mail you for another date. Trust me, if he likes you, he will ask you on a second date. End of story!

As opposed to directly asking him, "Will you call me?" the best way to hint that you'd be up for another date is to say, "I had a really nice time" at the end of the date. This will signal to him that it's okay to ask you out again, but it's his decision to do the asking. Try this as opposed to confronting him by saying "do you want to go out again?" Men hate confrontation.

Another acceptable option is to send him a quick text or e-mail after the date to say, "Thanks for dinner. I had a nice time." The key here is to not mention another date or pressure him to take you out again. By saying you had a nice time, it automatically lets him know that you enjoyed his company, and if he likes you he will ask you out again.

Lanny, and Tommy, and Brett, Oh My!

You're not paying, so it doesn't really matter how many men you date at once as long as you remember their names. Seriously, it's okay. The idea of dating more than one guy at once really bothers some women. They think it's dishonest, and that when they're dating someone, they need to give them their full attention 24/7. Yes, you might want to acknowledge his presence and slip a smile during the two hours you're sharing moo shu chicken over candlelight, but he really has no role in your life during the other 166 hours of the week. If you've been on one date with a guy, you really have no obligation to him besides saying, "Thank you. I had a great time." And if you think that one date with Lanny prevents you from sharing moo shu with Tommy, then you may be headed for trouble.

Ms. Avi's Reasons to Date More Than One Guy at Once:

✡ So you don't become obsessed over one guy.

✡ So he still has reasons to win you over.

✡ So your options are left open for you to meet a better guy. No wasting time; your eggs aren't getting any younger.

✡ So you don't see him more than one or two times a week in the beginning.

✡ For dating practice.

✡ To give your ego a boost with all that male attention.

✡ For free food.

✡ Did I mention that dating is fun?

WTF Are We?

Any decent God-fearing shiksa lets her man pace the relationship (while not allowing him to move too fast), and does not dare mention exclusivity too soon. In the beginning, date him unexclusively—with no pressure on him. During this time, your job is to be a fun happy-go-lucky girl, un-obsessed with marriage. Your job is to receive and to blissfully give the guy you're dating plenty of space. If you're a nice Jewish girl like Ms. Avi, then most of what I just described is a lie. Well, it's not a *lie*, it's just acting. But that's okay, put on your best shiksa hat and pretend.

One of the fun parts about dating is feeling those butterflies in your stomach when you don't know where a relationship stands. Once you've been out with a guy at least a month, you think he has *boyfriend* potential, and you're 50 percent sure he's free of erectile dysfunction—that is when you want to know if you're exclusive. But at the same time, you don't want to rush him. Let him take the lead on this issue, but if he never brings it up, there are two possible reasons:

1. He assumes you're exclusive, and thinks it's ridiculous to ask.
2. He doesn't want to be exclusive, but enjoys making out with you.

> Your man may assume that you're exclusive, but you should never take for granted that you are exclusive unless you ask. If you go on a date with him every Saturday night for two months, you probably are exclusive, but unless he tells you that, he may be shtupping Jessica on the nights you're not together. Ask him to be sure.

Many believe never to ask a guy, "What are we?" But the truth of the matter is that if he likes you, he wants to be the only guy sucking face with you; in other words, he wants to be your boyfriend. If he's never introduced you to his friends, it's a bad sign. Men want to show off what's theirs. He will show you off either because he truly loves you or because he thinks his friends will be jealous because you're hot. If he doesn't say within three months that he really likes you and wants to make it exclusive, it's a bad sign. If he says he doesn't want a relationship after three months, he will *never* want one with you. He may just be hanging out with you hoping to get some. If he doesn't feel a certain way about you, he won't want the baggage of having to call you on the phone or buy you pretty things. Therefore, you're just a glorified hooker to him.

Even though it's a vital conversation to have, Ms. Avi begs you not to ask on date three or four. Always wait a month or two before asking about relationship status. Bring out your inner shiksa and wait before bringing up exclusivity. It's better to find this out in two months than in six months, but it is necessary to give him those first few months of casual dating to make up his mind. If his response to your inquiry is, "You're a fun girl, but I'm not sure we should be exclusive yet," that's code word for, "You're hot, I like making out with you, but I would never take you home to meet my mother. In fact, I'd be embarrassed to introduce you to my dog." Time to move on, honey buns.

No Answer Is Your Answer:
A few months of dating is plenty of time for him to decide if he wants to be your boyfriend. In fact, his penis probably decided within five seconds of meeting you! If after getting to know you, he doesn't want to be your boyfriend, then he never will. But don't worry my sweet; the sooner you move on, the closer you are to finding a great new man.

Lauren was dating Greg on an every other weekend basis. She asked after four months, "Are we exclusive?" He said he needed a week to think about it. Red flag. After a week had passed, they were out at Fuddruckers celebrating her birthday (he was cheap), and his response to Lauren's question was, "It's not a good idea for us to be in a relationship." She was initially hurt, but now she's glad that she brought up the topic, or else she would have wasted more time with him (and potentially more birthdays at Fuddruckers).

If the man you're seeing does not bring up exclusivity after a few months, then it is *not* crazy-control-freak of you to ask. You deserve to know where you stand after a few months. If you bring up exclusivity and he gives you no answer or is unsure, then that is your answer. So what did we learn here? Fuddruckers on a birthday— red flag. More importantly, we learned that you should wait a few months, and if he hasn't brought up exclusivity, then you may bring it up so as to not waste your time.

Follow the dating advice in this chapter, and you'll have him fooled into thinking he's spending time with a down-to-earth shiksa who does not drop her life for a man. Dating rituals pace a relationship so that you make sure you're falling for the right person. Falling in love truly requires thinking with your head as well as following your heart. If you are not the right match, then pacing and dating rituals (and not immediately jumping into a relationship) will allow you to use your head to evaluate whether this is a relationship worth taking the time to pursue.

Dear Ms. Avi,
I have this device called a cell phone. Please help me use it!

Sincerely, Regina

Dear Regina,

The telephone was invented in the 1870's, and women have been abusing this technology ever since.

A man uses the phone to coordinate plans efficiently, get the job done, and move on with his day—not to yap for hours. When you call a man out of the blue who you are just getting to know, you may catch him off guard. It also puts him on the spot to ask you out. Maybe he hasn't figured out a plan yet for the next date? Unless you're dating a man exclusively, there is rarely reason to call unless you are returning a call.

So he called you, great! Here's a breakdown of how a phone call should be handled:

1. Chit chat for a few minutes
2. Allow him to ask you out and make plans
3. Come up with some excuse to get off the phone (dinner or the gym are good excuses)

If a man calls you, regardless of whether or not you are interested, it is polite to return his call. Many women will ignore a man's call hoping he will just kind of go away. Leaving him hanging is the worst way to treat someone. If you are not into him, just be upfront immediately and let him know that you are flattered, but not interested. That way, you do not end up with five more desperate-sounding messages on your phone (as amusing as it can be to re-play those for your girlfriends over and over again).

Your cell phone probably also has a functionality, popular among 12 yr old girls, called *texting*. Now, take notes...

Ms. Avi's Four Texting Guidelines:

1. Avoid engaging in long texting bouts. Follow this guideline on all men including those you have never met in-person (if met online) as well as the men you are dating. A guy once texted me 15 times without asking me out. What a time-waster he turned out to be!

2. If he texts you with a question such as "how was your big meeting today?" just simply reply back "it went great, everyone really loved my idea." Done. If you answer his text with a follow-up question, you are setting yourself up to engage in hours of texting which may or may not result in him *actually* asking you out.

3. Wait at least five minutes before answering his text messages.

4. Texting is best left for last-minute notes such as "running five minutes late."

Lastly, return a phone call with a phone call. Return a text with a text. Love, Ms. Avi

Chapter 6

Let Him Define the Relationship (Or at Least Let Him Believe That)

Once you have him wrapped around your finger and you're in an exclusive relationship, it's not the time to gain 20 pounds and throw out the flat iron. Now is the time to step into high gear to keep him hooked and eventually get the ring. This relationship phase is all about letting him have the space he needs to allow his love for you to grow. Here we'll discuss how to discern whether he loves you and treats you well, or if he's just wasting your time. If he's wasting your time, recognize it and get rid of him before your eggs get any older! For more on the evaluation process, please see Chapter 8.

Pace the Relationship Like a Shiksa:
My friend Sonia began dating a guy and within two weeks they were seeing each other five nights a week. After the one-month mark, he felt like his life had been taken over. A few weeks later, he broke it

off. Pacing a relationship could potentially be the difference between crying with a pint of Ben & Jerry's and eventually standing under the Chuppah—so take notes.

Space is essential if you want his love for you to blossom. If you see each other five nights a week in the beginning, there's nowhere to go but down. Not only will you deprive yourself of the time it takes to determine if he is right for you, but you'll end up wanting to see less of each other when you should want to see more of each other. A woman like you has a life outside of guys and does not have time to see one man five days a week. If he wants to see you three times a week, see him two, but try to see him at least once a week to keep the relationship's rhythm going. Men like rituals, so make it a ritual that you spend Saturday nights together or have Sunday brunch together. Obviously seeing someone once a week in a long-distance relationship may not be possible, but still do try to find a ritual of getting together every two weeks or once a month.

The other advantage of seeing him only once or twice a week in the beginning is that you can make sure that you look smokin' every time you see him, even if you're just sitting on his couch eating Chinese food. If you see him too often, you might get tired of primping for him, and he'll end up seeing you in your flannel fleece pajamas or retainer too soon and on a regular basis.

Men May Love Bitches, But Eventually He'll Want to See Your Nurturing Side:

When you first start dating a guy, Ms. Avi believes in being an irresistible, mysterious shiksa to potential suitors. You don't want to lie, but it is unnecessary to tell him on a second date about how you were anorexic in high school. Keep it light, and let more time pass before you disclose personal details about your life.

Once in a relationship, honesty and open communication are important (but not *too* much; he still doesn't want to hear about cramps). Remember, you're hoping to be the future mother of his children. The mother of his children shouldn't be an evil bitch. Once in a relationship, show him your Jewish mother side a bit. Prepare chicken soup if he's sick or break out the Neosporin when he scratches his knee playing basketball. Let him know he can trust you to be there for him through thick and thin.

Jewish Friendography and How to Not Be a Clinger:

We all know about Jewish Geography, but what about the fact that if you are both involved in Jewish life in your cities or universities, you will inevitably share some of the same friends? That's all fine and dandy during the relationship, but if it ends, you will want to ensure that the situation doesn't get sticky. You need to ensure that you have friends who were *your* friends first before you two got together. Otherwise, if you break up, the people who were his friends first will most likely align with him. So sad.

As important as it is to have separate friends from your boyfriend, you also need to ensure that you nurture those friendships while dating. Becoming wrapped up in a boyfriend and neglecting the rest of your life will lead you to being friendless. No respectable shiksa would ever drop everything in her life for a man, and neither should you. Pacing a relationship enables you to make and keep friends of your own—not so you can hook up with them when you break up, but because you need friends to start spreading evil rumors about him…oops, I meant to say be there for you.

Exhibit A is Jody, who transferred to my high school during junior year. She made a few female friends, but soon after, she began dating Charlie, and leached onto his friends. When they broke up, where were her friends to comfort her? They weren't there, because Jody didn't have any. They were all his friends, and were obviously allied with him. When you start dating someone new, don't drop your friends just because you now have someone to cuddle with at night. Your man will respect you more if you keep your own life going. Furthermore, giving a guy plenty of space is easy and natural when you have your own life full of sports, work, graduate school, political campaigns, and going to the gym.

No Need to Buy His Affection—The Shiksa Gift:

Oh, what a day of confusion a holiday or birthday can be when you're dating or in a relationship. In this case, less is more. One of the best gifts I ever gave a guy was a $15 mini blender. Unless you've been together for at least four months, taking him out for a romantic dinner on his birthday is overboard. On the other side of the spectrum, the *Shiksa Gift* says, "I care, but I'm not trying to buy your affection." What to get him all depends on how well you know him and how long you've been dating. Check out the box for advice on giving the perfect *Shiksa Gift*.

The Shiksa Gift Guidelines:

✡ No buying him a romantic dinner for his b-day unless dating for four months.

✡ The $10 Rule: $10 per month of dating allowed to be spent on a gift. For example, if you've been dating two months, then spend less that $20 on his gift.

✡ No buying/making anything lovey-dovey (cologne, underwear, candy, or anything heart-shaped). Kate once gave a guy she'd been dating for two months a framed picture of them for his birthday … great picture, bad idea. She could tell he was freaked out when she gave it to him. Less (and less romantic) is truly more in this case.

✡ Spend less than he would on you. You're not his sugar mama. Never go over $100 unless engaged or married.

Keep in mind, these guidelines are for *his* birthday. If he wants to take you out to a romantic dinner for your birthday…bring it on!

If you've only been out a few times, you can perhaps treat him to ice cream, rent a movie he would enjoy, or get him a card at most. If you've been dating a few months and are boyfriend/girlfriend, you could get him tickets to a hockey game or a bottle of his favorite alcohol, cook him dinner (which has the added benefit of letting him know you're comfortable in the kitchen), take him out to a restaurant he's been raving about, go to a concert, buy him a cool gadget, purchase a movie theater gift certificate, or give him sports team paraphernalia. There are so many options; just remember to stay within the guidelines of the *Shiksa Gift*.

Trust me, nowhere in the male brain exists the thought, "She didn't take me out for a romantic dinner. Who needs baseball tickets when I could have had a romantic dinner?"

Luckily, we're women (natural gold-diggers) and we care way more about what he gives us than he cares about what we give him. There's no way to forget V-day. The jewelry, lotion, candy, and card industries make it so that if he loves or cares about you at all, he couldn't possibly forget unless he lives in a hole, never goes out shopping, or doesn't own a TV. If he forgets about your birthday or V-day, it's not that he doesn't care for the holiday; it means he doesn't care about you. Something as simple as a single rose, a box of chocolates, or a dinner (just not Fuddruckers) shows that he loves/cares about you and sees more in the future of your relationship.

Mishpucha and the Two Jewish Mothers:

If you've been a good girl and paced the relationship like a shiksa, then there's rarely a reason to introduce a man to your family before three months or so have passed. Obviously, there are cases where there may be a graduation or bar-mitzvah involved, but do everything in your power to keep him and your family separated like milk and meat for the first few months. Your best bet may actually be to go dateless to the bar-mitzvah. Living at home with family?

Then have him pick you up outside the house so he does not have to be subjected to your mother.

> **Reasons to Wait to Introduce Him to Family:**
> 1. Who knows what the hell will come out of their mouths?
> 2. It automatically makes you more serious of a couple.
>   a. You still may need time to decide if he's the right person for you.
>   b. He may get scared that it's getting too serious too soon.

When is it okay to meet his family? Meeting a man's family is a very exciting time (unless it's at a funeral). Sometimes a man will jump in immediately and introduce you. Although this is a good sign that he sees you as more than a glorified hooker, be sure that you're comfortable with the situation and ready to meet his family—it's a big step. If he hasn't introduced you to anyone within 6 months of dating (parents, siblings, or cousins), then it's time to wonder why. Either they live too far away or he just doesn't see you as anything serious.

Now on to mom, the only member of his family worth noting. You may have assumed that this is the one part of a relationship where you stand at a significant advantage over the shiksa and you're home-free. Guess again. While it's true that when you first meet his mother, she will be happy just for the simple fact that you are Jewish, there may be some issues hidden from plain sight.

But before we can delve any further, we need to accept that there are two types of Jewish mothers:

1. The "as long as the girlfriend is Jewish and has a pulse" mother.
2. The "no one's good enough for my son" mother.

Now, type 1 is obviously easy to deal with. You still need to show her respect, but she is easier for you to woo than Lindsey Lohan to alcohol. Type 2 is oftentimes a woman who never had much of her own career and therefore needs to remain in control of her children. Now, here's where your shiksa appeal comes in handy...

A shiksa goes into meeting the mother thinking, "Oh my gosh, I am the cause of the destruction of the Jewish people; she's going to hate me." Therefore, from square one the shiksa knows she's walking on egg-shells and works super-hard to impress. She is polite, not overly opinionated, and knows she cannot give mom a single reason to discriminate against her.

If you approach a type 2 mother as you would a type 1 mother, you may make some fatal mistakes such as walking into their home as if you own the place, being over-confident, and not showing her the amount of respect she seems to think she deserves. The type 2 mom is out to prove she's the number one woman in her little boy's life and that she knows what's best for her son, even though she is probably the cause of his problems. Just play along and be polite. As for the rest of his family, just act nice, and you'll be in the clear.

Some Shiksa Techniques to Impress a Type 2 Mother:
- ✡ Compliment her clothing style or home.
- ✡ Write a thank-you note for a dinner or something she gave you.
- ✡ Find commonalities.
- ✡ Show that she's the boss when she's around him. Let her tell him what to do, not you.
- ✡ Pretend to respect her opinions.
- ✡ Bring her flowers if visiting her home.

"Dude...You're So Whipped":
Many Jewish men have heard this phrase from their friends, and it is one to avoid at all costs. If he wants to spend a weekend with the guys, let him, and be sure not to text him every 30 minutes. He will appreciate the space you give him and it will allow his love for you to grow.

How Much Crap Should I Leave at His Place?:
There is a very easy answer to this question: a shiksa leaves a little less than he invites her to leave. For example, if he tells you to leave a hair dryer, socks, and hairspray, then leave two out of the three items. Remember it's always better to be personally invited to the party as opposed to showing up uninvited. In other words, don't just start bringing stuff over and leaving it at his place. Wait for him to notice that you're wandering through the Egyptian desert carrying around an entire travel kit in your handbag. Unless he's completely oblivious, he'll eventually offer you a place to keep that girly deodorant.

Moving in and Hosting Shabbat Dinner Every Friday Night Together:
Moving in together can be a great decision if you are positive that he wants to marry you. Some women move in with a guy and use it as a *trial* period to see if they can stand living with a man, or to convince him to propose. But when she moves in, he's got everything he could ever want at his fingertips—sex, free cooked meals, and cleaning—but without kids or promising to give away half his assets in case of divorce. If your goal is to sign a ketubah with this man, then moving in will not make him propose more quickly. It may actually delay his proposal, because by moving in you make yourself too accessible and he does not have to fear losing you. What motivation does he now have to marry you?

The Ms. Avi Test to Determine Whether You Should Move in with Him:

Question #1: Has he said at some point, "[Insert your name here], I want to stand with you under a Chuppah someday and have you nag me for the rest of my life"?

Circle one:

Yes

No

Answer Key (this is a short test):

Yes: Ms. Avi gives you her blessing. You are free to move in together and to host many Shabbat dinners together.

No: If he hasn't said those words, or something of the sort, then you have absolutely no reason to move in together. If you're looking to save money, go to Craigslist and find a female roommate. She may not cuddle with you, but at least she's not wasting your time and leading you on (unless she owns four cats and scares away all the men from your apartment).

The age old question of whether he will propose stills eludes many women. A light bulb goes off in a man's mind when he wants to find a wife, and he morphs into a *Homing Pigeon*. The elusive *Homing Pigeon* is a man who reeks of wanting to get married. All his friends might be married, everything is about couples, and he is the one asking if you'd be alright settling in Scarsdale. Some men are natural Homing Pigeons and are ready for marriage at age twenty. Some, like Scott Baio, will shtup everything in sight and not be ready for marriage until forty-five, when they realize how unfulfilling the player lifestyle can be. He can't be pressured into wanting to get married; it's really the luck of the draw. How long do you wait around without a ring?

When you've been in a relationship with a guy for more than a year or two without a ring, you have two options:

A. You can tell him that you're looking for marriage and you want to know if it's going in that direction. Sometimes men aren't in the right place in their lives for weddings and pretty cakes. They may be in law school, or they may be looking for a job. Men want to feel secure before they propose, so they can best serve their role as providers.

B. Or you can waste five years waiting for him to propose without knowing whether he has any intention of proposing—ever. He will enjoy your company and sex, and hopefully he will buy you some pretty, shiny jewelry. But the one piece of jewelry you want, a ring, has eluded you. After those five years, you are older and less attractive. Don't let him waste your precious time.

But there's one part of the relationship we've neglected to discuss...

Chapter 7 —

Be the Preacher's Daughter: Sex, Sin, and Recognizing the Kosher Player

Last fall, I set up my two friends Tamara and Marc. They had a nice first date, and on the second date he invited her over to watch a movie. Now, his roommate was deeply entrenched in a game of *Halo* in the living room, so they had to watch in his bedroom. Naturally, it wasn't just a movie. Later, Tamara had no idea if any of the *American Pie* kids got any play with anything other than apple pie, because she spent the last hour of the movie sucking face with Marc. Tamara liked him, but he was simply bored, and she happened to be on his bed. It just seemed obvious to him that they would make out—no strings attached.

Being the good yenta that I am, I asked Marc what he thought of Tamara. He replied, "I didn't feel any chemistry, but I made out with her anyway because she was there." Like any respectable girl, Tamara was hurt and confused when she never heard from him again. She called me and asked, "Why would he kiss me if he didn't like me?" I told my naïve friend that men don't get emotional over the physical aspects of a relationship as easily as women. They have this evil ability to separate sex from emotions. Lucky sons of bitches.

There's a book called *The Kosher Sutra* for a reason; Judaism is a very sexual religion. It's a mitzvah to *have a good time* with your wife on the Sabbath, and married women cover their hair in order to save it for their husbands. The laws of Niddah (or separation) strengthen the physical bond and desire between a married couple. These laws keep an Orthodox husband and wife apart for a minimum of 12 days per month during and after the woman's period. No touching, no sleeping in the same bed, and unfortunately no mud wrestling during this part of the month.

The majority of this chapter does not apply to Orthodox Jews, but applies to Reform or Conservative Jewish girls who have a reputation for giving up sex very easily to any guy with "stein" in his last name. This chapter will look into the different ways men and women view sex, explore how to challenge men, and we'll take a few pointers from the shiksiest of all shiksas, the preacher's daughter.

A Change in Definition:

For generations, the shiksa has been linked to the forbidden sexual desires of young Jewish men. These men may have grown up in entirely Jewish communities where the tall, blonde shiksa was an exotic prize to be won. Don't get me wrong; there still are Jewish men who use shiksas as sexual toys. But in today's melting pot, sex is all too easy and acceptable, and a man no longer needs a shiksa goddess for this. Jewish women are down for a good time as well—but is that helping or hurting us?

The good-Christian shiksa who does not give away the goodies easily is actually more dangerous than the promiscuous shiksa, because she will hook a man and take him to the altar. As a nice Jewish girl, your job is to challenge him, bait him, and not give into his desires immediately. This is where we can learn from the preacher's daughter.

The preacher's daughter doesn't compromise her morals to impress a guy. In fact, because the shiksa does not give in to his desires immediately, she creates even more desire, until he's singing "White Christmas" with her family. A Jewish girl may try so hard to reel in a nice guy that she ends up giving him access to the babka in her underpants too easily, while today's shiksa would not find herself in a situation of physical contact before she is comfortable.

By pretending to be an inexperienced Christian girl, the shiksa provides a challenge to her unsuspecting prey and he is lured in by the possibility of taking her virginity. Men thrive on challenge; they want to think that the girl they date or marry made them work for it. They want you to push back and not to give in to moving the relationship too fast sexually. Note: there is a significant difference between resisting the urge to pounce on him immediately and being afraid and uncomfortable about sex and your own body image. Jewish girls also have a reputation for being uncomfortable and prudish, so make sure to project body confidence and your belief in not giving it away to anyone and everyone. That is sexy.

Hold Off as Long as You Can:
Like our shiksa friends, keep it PG-rated for as long as possible. Although at some point, all men (if straight) will eventually want to do more with you physically than merely discuss congressional politics. Also consider the possibility that you're with a Kosher Player in disguise who pretends for a few weeks to like you, but really only wants to get with you. When a man sees a future with a woman, he does not rush into sex, because he fears scaring her off. Ms. Avi's four main reasons for holding off on the physical aspects of the relationship are:

1. **You (a female) cannot separate the physical from the emotional:**
   Men are able to differentiate between sex and emotions. Women usually develop a stronger emotional attachment for a man once they have slept together and may hold onto an unsuccessful relationship because they think they are more compatible than they really are. After you sleep with a man, you may end up feeling emotionally attached to him, while he may feel less attraction toward you now that the chase is over. Perhaps he never even felt anything for you to begin with!

2. **A challenge holds his interest:**
   Easy girls are, well…easy. They are also not long-term potential girls. You are. Refer back to Chapter 2 for other techniques to challenge him.

3. **I like him…oh wait, I'm not sure:**
   As crazy as this sounds, it's not all about him. We're looking to find you a loving man and therefore another reason to pace the relationship is that it's difficult to tell if a guy's right for you if you get physical too quickly. After having sex, the vast majority of women will inevitably feel a stronger attraction towards a man. It is quite possible that the physical attraction and the emotions that come with sex could mask they fact that he is not compatible with you. By holding off on the physical, you can make a fair and honest assessment of whether he is indeed just a douchebag. Allow yourself the time to really get to know him as a person.

4. **Weeding out Kosher Players:**
   If you do not give a Kosher Player what he wants immediately, he will either get bored, disgruntled, or just leave. If a man

pressures you too much, you may have a Kosher Player on your hands whose bedroom has seen more action than Ellis Island in the early 1900's.

The Green Signal:

Like Tamara, some women mistake a man's physical advances for deep attraction or use kissing and sex as an attempt to lure a man their way. The classic error many women make is displaying the Green Signal, a sign to a man that you want some action, too soon. If a chick displays the Green Signal, she may get physical only to find out that he just made out with her because "she was there." If this signal is displayed, a man may try to get as much as he can, even from a girl that's a four on the looks scale. This doesn't make him a bad person; it just means he's not gay.

Ms. Avi's Guide to Avoiding the Green Signal:

If you put yourself in a situation like the ones listed below, you automatically give a man the Green Signal. Follow the guidelines below to keep yourself out of trouble if it's too early in the relationship to get physical.

- ✡ Stay on the couch. Beds send the wrong message.
- ✡ Don't talk about sex. If you do, he will perceive that you are down for a good time.
- ✡ Don't grind against him.
- ✡ Leave if he gets too friendly.
- ✡ Don't spend the night.

Note: This list does not apply to Israeli soldiers, because everything is a Green Signal to them.

Leslie once found herself in a situation where she inadvertently gave the Green Signal to her friend, Kyle, a guy she hoped to date in the future. She had a little too much Sangria at a Cinco de Mayo fiesta, and Kyle offered to take her back to his place since she was in no condition to drive home. She accepted the invitation to get cozy on his couch. She thought she was just there to sleep, but he thought she slept there on purpose. At 2 a.m., he went over to the couch and began rounding second base. When she stopped him, he became disgruntled and called her a prude. Men really do get upset when they see that green light turning red (even nice guys). Leslie could have avoided the Green Signal by having a girlfriend drive her home from the party.

The issue with the Green Signal is that it can potentially halt a budding relationship or it might cause you to go further faster than you intended. Don't be labeled a tease, avoid the Green Signal.

Sexy Time Kosher Style Q&A:

Here Ms. Avi attempts to answer the age-old question: should you engage in physical intimacy? How will his opinion of you change? How long before he leaves you for a girl who puts out? Many a shiksa has pulled the, "I'm a good Christian and I'm waiting for marriage" BS line and has ended up under a Chuppah with one of our tribesmen. It's not necessarily that these smart and coy women ever intended to wait for marriage, but they were perceived as a *challenge* by the men who ended up taking their virginity.

Q: How long should I wait to see his Hebrew National™?

A: All women have their own definition of what "waiting" means. A month may be waiting for you, but may be too fast for him. The last thing you want is a man thinking that he didn't have to work or spend a few shekels to get you. By insisting that you wait until you're dating exclusively, he'll keep the impression that you are selective about who you sleep with.

A good rule of thumb is to wait until he calls you his *girlfriend* or until you know for a fact that you're the only girl who's seen the inside of his bedroom for at least a few weeks. If he says, "I expect sex by the third date," lose him; he doesn't care about you. Three dates isn't enough time to figure out how you feel about him. If he gently pushes to move further, that's normal, as long as he doesn't threaten to leave.

Q: How experienced should I pretend to be?

A: Men who are sexually active prefer a woman with some experience, but what they don't want is a woman who sleeps around and might carry diseases. Guys yearn to feel superior in their prowess and to appear that they know what they're doing. In his mind, you should be that innocent preacher's daughter who he can teach a thing or two. If you come into the bedroom with skills like Barbara Streisand on stage, then you will emasculate him and he will no doubt wonder if you messed around with every guy in your Hebrew school class back in the day.

The take-home message here is to act as if you're slightly less experienced than he is (depending on age). For instance, if you're twenty-three and dating a thirty-year-old, of course it's normal for you to act less experienced than he is. But if you're both twenty-seven, and he's slept with five girls, then naturally you'd say you've slept with three guys. Let him think he's a macho man (like Jeff Goldblum), and you're that nice Jewish girl with slightly less experience.

Q: What if I plan on waiting until marriage?

A: If you're an observant Jew, then this entire book has probably offended you, and I'm sorry. You can completely ignore the chapter until here. Also, the parts about Asian women stealing your men probably don't apply to you. Okay, back to my point: people wait for marriage for a variety of reasons—some personal, some religious. If you are looking for an Orthodox man, then you, too, should wait for marriage. I'm not one to sugarcoat, and the truth is that many secular men today don't prefer virgins, but many of them would wait a long time if they met the right girl and she preferred to wait. Just as some Jews like Gefilte Fish while others would rather eat a pigeon, some guys like virgins and some don't. So if it's for religious or personal reasons that you're waiting for marriage, then you should feel comfortable that waiting is the right decision.

In summary, you don't earn his love by putting out. You earn his love by being yourself—and showing cleavage. If that doesn't work, then he's not the one for you. Kosher Players are very good at coercing women into their apartments or beds. But hopefully you have enough self-esteem and a pet *Rabbit* at home to help you save the goodies for a man who treats you with respect. As we learned from our shiksa friends, challenge is the key to hooking a man. Let him work a little before you get physical. But don't fret, my pet; you can still pique his interest without putting out too much. Oftentimes for men, the thought and anticipation of sex is more motivating and powerful than the actual physical encounter.

Dear Ms. Avi,
Is there anything wrong with a hooking up with a guy on a continual
basis if we're not technically dating?
Diana

Dearest Diana,
He may be an ex-boyfriend, someone you had a crush on in eighth grade, or your soccer coach. Hooking up cheapens sex. It's a great deal for him—he has no biological clock. As long as the equipment is in working order, he's good to go.

Pros:

✡ Makes you act less on-edge and less desperate when you meet a guy you do like.

Cons:

✡ It makes it less meaningful for you when you do find that special someone.

✡ If you're in public, it looks like you have a boyfriend, so other guys will be less inclined to approach you.

✡ It stops you from going out and meeting other guys (if you're spending your Friday nights with him).

✡ It lessons the pressure for him to go out and find a new girl. And remember, us Jewish chicks are trying to help each other out. From his perspective, why date and spend money on other ladies when he's already getting it for free?

✡ If you are attracted to him physically or emotionally, you may be tricking yourself into thinking you're in a relationship. A relationship may be the furthest thing from his mind.

Remember, men are perfectly happy to use you without wanting to take you home to Mom. If you do decide to engage in this behavior, keep it to a once-in-a-while meeting as opposed to a continual rendezvous with emotional attachment. That way, it doesn't inhibit either of you from finding perfect Jewish matches. As my friend Rob says, "Just go buy a toy—don't cheapen yourself."

Love, Ms. Avi

Chapter 8—

Evaluate Like the Shiksa: Is He Actually your Prince Mensching?

Sometimes it's easy to think that there's no one better than [insert name here] out there for you, but even if he's a perfect mate on paper, it's time to get out if you feel like crap on a regular basis. I know; breaking up is scary stuff. Thoughts of dying alone watching reruns of *Days of Our Lives* may cross your mind—and let's not forget having to tell Aunt Verna at Passover that you're single again. On the other hand, dating, going out for free meals, and new relationship butterflies are all really exciting. You're not getting any younger, so as soon as you put on your shiksa hat, objectively evaluate, and realize that he's not your future husband, get out.

You may never find anyone as good looking or as rich as he is, but you will find someone who's a better fit for you—someone who treats you like his Jewish Princess. So, how do you decide to call it quits with a guy whose Italian cooking is to die for or? Read on, buttercup.

Ms. Avi's List of Factors That Matter:

Many women, in their quest for perfection, will dismiss a man based purely on trivial factors. Such factors could include the types of movies he likes, the way he holds a fork, or his fashion sense. A shiksa knows that these qualities are trivial. Does the way he holds his fork on a date mean that he won't be a loyal husband who loves you unconditionally when you're eighty and wearing an adult diaper and a purple sequined matching sweat suit?

Some women go so far as to write laundry lists of all the qualities they're looking for in a man. A true shiksa would write no such ridiculous list. These lists are often too picky, too unrealistic, and these women will be single until they're fifty unless they get a grip on the Jewish singles' market. You need to honestly evaluate yourself, estimate your market price, and set realistic standards in your search for an ideal partner. Are the really good looking, successful guys lining up to ask you out? The qualities you should be looking for in a man are long-term partner potential and whether he's the future father of your children. No matter whether you're a gold-digging bitch like me or a really sweet girl, consider the bullet points below in making your decision:

✡ **Money to Pay for Your Child's Bar-Mitzvah:** In the long-run, can he support you financially so that you live a comfortable lifestyle? If you're like Ms. Avi and go for the lawyers, the answer to that question should be *yes*. Does he have direction and passion for his career? I like to say that a man should either make a lot of money or have passion for his work. Even if you're married to a teacher who's making sixty thousand a year, if he has passion for his students (just not *too* much passion…), then he's a keeper.

✡ **Seriously Bad Habits, Proceed with Caution:** Major gambling, alcoholism, drugs, smoking—these all could potentially signal danger. No one's perfect, so if he does have addictions, make sure you're okay with his issues, or find a new guy. These addictions usually don't just magically go away (even by praying to Jesus), so make sure he gets help before you reproduce. Once kids are in the picture, you don't need Aba coming home with a 40 and a five-dollar hooker.

✡ **Minor Faults, Nothing to Plotz Over:** As I said before, no one's perfect. There's a distinct difference between stupid habits and dangerous addictions. If he's not always clean, hire a cleaning lady when you're married. If he makes a mess on the couch, take a tip from grandma, and line it with plastic. If he's chronically late, tell him to be ready fifteen minutes before the time he needs to be. These are all minor annoying issues, not deal breakers.

✡ **Does He Consider Eating a Bagel Practicing Judaism?** Last Yom Kippur, did you have to pull a crab cake out of his mouth? Or instead, did he judge you because you drank soda with corn syrup during Passover? Obviously, you're not going to find someone with the exact same religious views as you, but you need someone at least on the same page for the sake of future little baby Moshe. If you both watch Woody Allen movies or go to Temple the same amount (whether it's always, never, or just on the High Holy Days) and he's not waving around a Palestinian flag, then it sounds like you're generally on the same page and your kids will not be screwed up. (Okay, newsflash: you're Jewish and your kids will be Jewish, so there's a high probability they're gonna be weird and/or screwed up anyway. But it makes us special and unique.)

✡ **Where to Live and How Many Mouths to Feed:** Is his family in Los Angeles, and he wants to move back there for the tan blondes and materialistic culture when he's done with law school? Does he want a boatload of children to start a choir, but you want only one? Ensure your life plans align in terms of where you want to settle and how many kids you want. These are discussions to have before you end up brokenhearted when a two-year relationship fizzles out.

✡ **Treats You Like a Princess:** You want to be important in his life. If you're important to him, he will contact you on a regular basis via phone, e-mail, or text. It will be his pleasure to do small things for you. Does he bring you nice stuff, call you, e-mail you, and ask you out? If he says, "I'm falling in love with you," but then only calls every other week, reconsider how much he means what he says. If he's hot and cold with you now, then he'll be even colder in marriage. Women sometimes accept the ring thinking that a man's faults will disappear when he gets married and that he will suddenly turn into Prince Mensching. How he treats you while you're dating is how he will treat you in marriage. Find one who treats you well.

✡ **Drop It Like It's Hot:** It's been proven that marriages are more likely to last longer when a woman is more attractive than her man. Keep in mind, though, that beauty is in the eye of the beholder. If he's with you, and he pursued you, then he thinks you're hot. Don't let him smell your fear. Act as if you never noticed that objectively he could be an underwear model. (I don't know any Jewish guys who are, though, so if you do, please introduce me.) As long as he *thinks* you're hotter than he is, he'll treat you like a queen forever and that's all that matters.

✡ **The Mediocre Kosher Sutra:** The important question here is not whether you're using whips and chains, but whether you enjoy being intimate with your boyfriend. Good sex is good enough. Just be happy you're getting some.

From Ms. Avi's List of Factors that Matter, you need to decide what's a deal breaker to you. If it's time for him to go and for you to hit up awkward Jewish singles events, then so be it!

Time to Part Like the Red Sea?

So you've been dating for a few months or a year and are a little unsure about him or his income. You may sit around waiting for *him* to break it off, but here's a newsflash that every good shiksa knows: you're better off doing it and not waiting for him. People of the male species are perfectly happy to date you even if there's no ring in your future. Men hear their faux biological clocks ticking when they're forty because by then they only have a few years to find a ripe thirty-year-old woman to make babies with. You might be harassed for years by your overly anxious mother about "letting that one get away." Forget her—get out of that dead-end relationship now and get yourself to the next speed-dating event.

Your Eggs, Wasting Time, and Vasectomies:

In your twenties, you're at the height of the dating totem pole. Even the men who were too good for you in high school are starting to drool over you. But don't let this newfound hotness go to your head. This is not the time to be adamant about finding a six-foot-tall athletic investment banker. The time between twenty and thirty is when you can have fun but should not waste time searching for the holy grail that doesn't exist. If the right one comes along, hold on and don't let go!

If you haven't met your match by thirty-five, that's when you have to really bring your A-game. There are still many good men for you; you just have to pretend to be that un-bitter, not marriage obsessed, happy go lucky shiksa. As Lori Gottlieb, author of *Marry Him: The Case for Settling for Mr. Good Enough*, says, "A half shelf life for a woman is about thirty-five. The real shelf life is forty. Once you're forty and dating online, no guy who wants to have kids is willing to even meet you. Divorced guys who already have kids will meet a forty-year-old, but many of them have had vasectomies." This by no means that you have to throw in the towel at 35 or even 40—many people still find love after 40. However, your dating pool has to be expanded to include divorced men who potentially have children.

It's fine in high school to play around and to even date a guy for years knowing that he's not the one. When you're thirty, though, if he's not right within four months, you really don't have a lot of time to mess around. A true man who's ready to get married and procreate, aka a *Homing Pigeon*, will at some point bring up the future, kids, or marriage. But if he doesn't mention these topics directly, all is not lost—pay attention to ways he may do so without being obvious. He may talk about his brother's upcoming wedding, the large townhouse he's thinking of buying that he can "grow into," the fact that he wants to settle down in New Jersey, or his recent visit to see his new nephew. These are hints that he may be a *Homing Pigeon* in disguise that aren't as obvious or as desperate-sounding. But if he's not sending these signals your way....

Wasting years with a man who is not marriage material is un-shiksa-like and is unacceptable. Your friends will not sympathize with you by saying, "Oh, I'm so sorry you spent eight years with a guy who never proposed." Sorry, that's your own fault! Even if you're twenty-seven and having a great time and lots of fun with a guy who has made it clear he has no intention of marrying you, you need to stop dating him exclusively. Go on JDate, join activities, clubs, sports, speed-dating, anything—just meet and date men with marriage potential! Think about your future and how your value as a female is plummeting as we speak. If you do have a great time with him, see him occasionally (no more than once a week) so you have time to date other men. Having men on the side is a great way to keep yourself from acting desperate, because you always have someone there on the back burner (and guys always want the girl who's wanted by others). Just keep it non-exclusive, so he's not preventing you from meeting someone great.

A Special Shout Out to the Baldies:
As we have stated before, baruch hashem that Jewish men seem to go bald at a higher rate than everyone else. If it weren't for male-pattern baldness, they would all remain playboys until death, none would marry other Jews, and our race would die out. If you see a guy who's balding, then it's a great time to start a relationship with him, because his ego will be taking a blow. You can be the sexy vixen who makes him feel young like a Fabio-stein (but obviously without all the hair). Not attracted to the Yul Brynner look? Just remember that the man you marry may eventually go bald anyway, so make yourself attracted to that look!

If He Calls It Quits:
I'm going to keep this short and sweet. If a guy dumps you, it means he doesn't want to marry you. Period. Move on to find guys who *do* want you (and they're out there). In Judaism, we are encouraged to question. Do the opposite here. Just accept that for some reason or another, he's not the one for you. If he were, he'd be saving up his money for a ring. What Ms. Avi does encourage is self-evaluation to determine in which departments you could use some sprucing up (whether it's looks, physique, awkwardness, target shooting, or knowledge of wine pairings) for the next guy. They say it takes half the time of a relationship to get over a guy. Well if that were true, we'd all die alone as old maids.

The Shiksafied Break-Up Plan:

1. Take time to be in pain: Let the emotions out (just not to him). Call or see friends, go to church (wait, I mean synagogue; we don't need to take the shiksa thing *that* far...), and go to the gym or on a walk.

2. Get the closure you need (optional): Sometimes in order to move on, you must talk it over with the guy. This is obviously different for each situation, but for instance, if he broke up with you and you're not sure why and it's really making you upset, just calmly call him and ask what went wrong. You may have gotten the answers you need while you were breaking up. If you broke up with him, this step may not be necessary.

3. Treat yourself well: Go get a massage, go to the gym every day, and go shopping for sexy clothes. Get yourself ready for the excitement of dating again.

4. Put yourself back on the market: The best cure for a break-up is newfound male attention. Put on that sexy shiksa outfit, refer back to Chapters 3 and 4, and get back out there.

When you go out with new guys, don't mention your ex (or any other guys for that matter) on the date. Just pretend to be happy, and eventually you will be. Avoid bitching excessively to your friends—they will eventually stop pretending to care and will ignore you—and then you will have nothing except that bag of Fritos and five extra pounds around your midline. Look at it as a positive: "He is not your beshert. Your beshert is still out there." Go find him! Feel bad about putting yourself out there too soon? Don't. He doesn't have a limited supply of eggs and a biological clock ticking away as we speak, and you do. Don't be afraid to tone up at the gym, re-join Weight Watchers for the third time, or go to the Clinique make-up counter for a free makeover.

If You De-Mensched:

If you broke his heart, you're probably having many of the same feelings as you would if he dumped you. Follow the plan above. You may question if you made the right decision to de-mensch yourself, and of course you're not sure when you will re-mensch. Your may be thinking about that beautiful Jewish wedding you wanted with him, breaking the glass under the Chuppah, and that Cuisinart food processor on your Williams Sonoma registry that never would have been taken out of the box. But if you're not right for each other or if he doesn't treat you how you deserve to be treated, then the decision was for the best. You'll get your food processor with another man who is a better match—and maybe you'll even use that food processor. Objective evaluation of your man can be a difficult process, but if he's not right for you, you must move on.

Dear Ms. Avi,
Can you tell me the best way to break up with my guy?

Thanks!
Anna

Dear Anna,
Well, that depends on how long you've been dating. Whatever your situation may be, remember in every Jewish community (I don't care if it's in New York City or Birmingham, Alabama), word gets around ... fast. Sooner or later, you're going to bump into him at a Shabbat dinner, run to the bathroom, and say, "Shit, I treated that guy like crap, and now he's friends with all the cute ones!" You also aim to dump with dignity because you don't want him thinking, "I hate all Jewish girls." Instead, you want him to say, "I dated a great chickadee, but we weren't meant for each other." If you give him a negative image of Jewish ladies, six months later, he'll be giving a shiksa a two-carat ring!

The best position to leave it is on friendly terms, so that way when you go up to him at an event, he can and will be happy to introduce you to his cute friends instead of telling them what a whore you are (which might attract them, you never know).

Here's how to break up or let him know he is not the future father of your children:

✡ 0–3 dates: If he's asked you out, but you'd rather spend time cleaning the toilet than going out, you can e-mail him with:

113

Dear Mordecai,
Thank you for taking me out last night. I enjoyed our
conversation about Joe Lieberman. I don't think that we're
right for each other, and I wish you the best of luck in your
MBA program. I think you're a great guy.
Best wishes, Anna

Or you can tell him over the phone if you have the guts.
(I have none; that's why I use e-mail.)

✡ 4 dates–4 weeks: Phone or in-person. Follow the steps
   from dates 0–3, but pretend to care a little more.

✡ 4 weeks–2 months: Phone or in-person. Say how much
   you care about him and how much you've enjoyed
   getting to know him, (blah, blah, blah…) but that
   you don't see it working out long term. Not enough in
   common, no spark, not going in the same direction. Just
   be sure to give him a reason.

✡ 2 months +: Same as above, but in-person. That's the
   least he deserves after all the money he's spent on you.

Also, I feel compelled to emphasize that if you are not
interested in a man, the best option is to let him know immediately.
Stringing a man along is cruel. So many women will simply wait
for him to realize she's not interested. Many guys can't take
hints…at all, so you really need to spell it out sometimes.

Love always, Ms. Avi

Concluding Thoughts

As much as I'd like to have spent the past eight chapters and semi-relevant intro blaming shiksas for former Hebrew school all-stars running astray, I cannot. It's a fact of life in today's American melting pot that Jewish men are going to date and marry Gentile women. Instead, we've delved into how to make yourself into the most succulent Jewish lady you can be and techniques to coerce Jewish men to date within their kind. By studying shiksa behavior and modifying our dating strategies, we, too, can attract quality Jewish men.

Marrying within the faith and raising Jewish children are the most important steps you can take in preserving our religion, heritage, and culture. It's cute that old people are at synagogue, but it's really about the youth, the future. Without Jewish children, there is neither continuity nor hope. Marrying within the faith is bigger than just satisfying your mother; it's about ensuring the future of our beautiful shared heritage.

Hopefully you'll walk away from this book with a renewed sense of pride for our shared traditions, a craving for a bagel, and a game plan for finding love. While doing so, it's imperative to keep in mind the following:

✡ Dating and mating are tough work. Finding a suitable Jewish man is no cakewalk, either. Put in the effort now while you're younger because …

✡ Your stock only goes down as you age (unless you lose weight or get plastic surgery).

✡ Treat your body and soul with respect; only give time to men who respect you.

✡ Believe that you're sassy, sexy, and worthy of a great man. You will find him.

Ditch that "perfect mensch" list. Perfect Jewish men do exist, but unfortunately they are either dating shiksas or have overblown egos. Your goal should be to live in a way that attracts quality men. It's about the attitude as much as the look. Dress femininely to accentuate your sexiness and minimize flaws, act calm, cool, and collected around men you find attractive, and put yourself in situations where there are men to meet. These will all enhance your ability to attract quality men. Don't think of it as your dating circle is limited to short balding Jewish guys, but instead that only Jewish men have the privilege of dating you.

And how did it end with my ex-boyfriend Adam, the former Hebrew school playboy-turned-shiksa-chaser? Last time I checked the "Book of Faces," he was

Wait for it …

Wait for it …

He was dating a girl named Michelle who went to Brandeis! Phew, close call there. Maybe I didn't turn him off from Jewish girls after all; I just made him work a little harder to realize that we are hot shit.

When I started this book, I was single, dating a lot of guys, and constantly accused by my friends of being the crazy cat lady minus the cats who went around giving dating advice. Now I sit here and speak to you having accomplished the nearly impossible— convincing a sweet and successful man (who had previously dated only shiksas) to fall for Ms. Avi, a *sometimes* nice Jewish girl.

Selected Bibliography and Recommended Reading

1. Argov, Sherry. *Why Men Marry Bitches: A Woman's Guide to Winning Her Man's Heart*. New York: Simon and Schuster, 2006.
2. Benvenuto, Christine. *Shiksa: The Gentile Woman in the Jewish World*. New York: St. Martin's Press, 2004.
3. Deyo, Yaacov, and Sue Deyo, Sue. *Speed Dating: The Smarter, Faster Way to Lasting Love*. New York: William Morrow, 2002.
4. Fein, Ellen, and Sherrie Schneider. *The Rules*. New York: Grand Central Publishing, 1996.
5. Fein, Ellen, and Sherrie Schneider. *The Rules II*. New York: Grand Central Publishing, 1998.
6. Fein, Ellen, and Sherrie Schneider. *The Rules for Online Dating*. New York: Gallery, 2002.
7. Furman, Leah. *Single Jewish Female*. New York: Perigee Trade, 2004.
8. Gottlieb, Lori. *Marry Him: the Case for Settling for Mr. Good Enough*. Boston: Dutton Adult, 2010.

9. Girsh, Kristina, Boy Vey!: *The Shiksa's Guide to Dating Jewish Men*. New York: Simon Spotlight Entertainment, 2005

10. Lipper, Jodi and Cerina Vincent. *Live Like a Hot Chick*. New York: Avon, 2010

11. Strauss, Neil. *The Game: Penetrating the Secret Society of Pickup Artists*. New York: It Books, 2005.

12. Uscher-Pines, Lori. *The Get-Your-Man-to-Marry-You Plan*. New York: St. Martin's Press, 2008